Longevity Insurance for a Biological Age

*Why your retirement plan shouldn't be based
on the number of times you circled the sun.*

Moshe A. Milevsky, Ph.D.

ISBN (softcover): 9781-7906-58268

First Printing: 12 March 2019

Dedicated to the memory of Joel Diena (1935-2019).
An Italian economist, doting dad, witty grandfather,
and most kindhearted person we ever knew.

AGE (Noun*)

[1]. The length of an existence extending from the beginning to any given time.

[2]. A cultural period marked by the prominence of a particular item.

<u>Source:</u> *Webster's Dictionary

TABLE OF CONTENTS

PROLOGUE

I am often asked by friends and colleagues *how* I got interested in the topic of annuities – which is admittedly a rather obscure subset of economics, insurance and actuarial science. Considering that I have been publishing articles about annuities for over a quarter of a century, it's not an unreasonable query. After all, what 20-year-old cares about these (old) things?

Well, if I can trace my long-standing interest in – and dare I say passion or even obsession with – annuities to some distant affair, I would trace the origins to two distinct events, both of which took place while I was researching and writing my Ph.D., in graduate school. The first incident was rather amusing – in hindsight, of course – and rather trivial compared to the second one, but both of them had far-reaching implications.

I'll start with the light-hearted one. Back in the early 1990s, when I was a young graduate student in Toronto, I wrote a term paper for an investment finance course that eventually became a published article entitled "How to Avoid Outliving Your Money." In that paper I used some fancy mathematics to investigate something called drawdown strategies. Think of someone with an initial sum of money – for example, a new retiree with no employment income – who is trying to maintain a desired standard of living. The relevant technical question is: How should they allocate a portfolio of stocks and bonds? Remember, this work was for a graduate investment course in a business school.

The key message in the article – which in the early 1990s might have appeared novel and fresh – was that a hypothetical retiree should continue to maintain a substantial exposure to stocks well into their 70s and 80s, because they were likely to *live* a long time. Technically speaking, the article proved that the *lifetime ruin probability*

(LRP) was minimized with more stocks versus bonds, assuming certain analytic mathematical properties, etc. Anyway, that was the main thesis and, like all budding academics in training, I decided to take the message on the road. Toronto is a cold place in winter, so I submitted the paper to a conference scheduled to take place somewhere warm, and an academic meeting of insurance actuaries in Orlando fit the bill.

So, in one of my very first ever public forays, I presented the above-mentioned technical paper to a large conference of insurance industry specialists. Well, the response from the crowd was tepid at best, partially because of my naiveté and inexperience with public speaking in front of large and diverse crowds. At the time, 25-year-old me believed that a room full of 50-year-old financial service professionals in Orlando would be nothing short of thrilled to experience a compendium of equations early in the morning after a night of social cocktails.

When I completed my symphony of Greek and the patient moderator asked the audience for questions, there weren't any from the floor. I remember this part clearly – you always remember your first – because after a long and awkward silence, someone, finally, lumbered over to the microphone and declared in a crisp British accent: "Young man, if what you are trying to do is reduce the probability of running out of money, then you should consider purchasing an annuity from a life office." There were murmurs, widespread nods of approval, some giggles from the audience and no other comments or questions. At the time my own mumbled response was that well, thank you for the great comments about annuities, and that I would have to look into that annuity thing carefully and thank you again, blah, blah.

You see, back then (1993, to be precise) I had absolutely no idea how a life annuity provided *longevity insurance* or protection against outliving wealth. It wasn't part of my curriculum in business school, or the established cannon in graduate courses on econometrics, micro-economics and derivative pricing. Yes, I learned everything there was to know about stocks, bonds, cash, commodities and various derivatives, but nothing about how one can place them inside an annuity "wrapper" and enhance them with mortality credits – something I'll explain later on. Even to this day, a proper understanding of annuities is not part of the formal educational curriculum for most college and university students in finance, economics and business. Many in the press and media still don't understand them either. But one thing is for certain, that humbling experience in front of hundreds of insurance actuaries in Orlando helped usher me into the world of annuities. I promised myself I wouldn't be embarrassed by annuities ever again.

The second incident – which jolted me into the field of protecting against life and death – is a far more serious and personal one.

My Longevity Risk

Around the same time, while I was in graduate school, my father – who at the time was just shy of 50 years old – was diagnosed with colon cancer, despite its absence in our family history. The illness eventually metastasized to his lung and liver. He died very soon afterwards, leaving five children, with me being the oldest. While this isn't the proper place to delve into the behavioral or psychological impact of losing your dad at such a young age, we were quite fortunate to have a very supportive family, and I got particularly close to my grandfather, who became a father figure of sorts.

Grandpa had grown up and was schooled in Germany, had left Europe just prior to World War II, and immigrated to the U.S. soon after. *Zeydy* (as we all fondly called him) was very supportive during those difficult years, while I was a graduate student working on my thesis. He was there with me at the convocation ceremony when I received my Ph.D. and I was fortunate to share many more years with him. He lived into his 90s.

That was the longevity paradox under which I lived.

My father barely made it into his 50s. My grandfather made it to his 90s. That is a longevity gap of 40 years. How does a family cope with this randomness? How can insurance protect against these risks? What are the financial implications? I have grappled with these sorts of question for half of my 50 chronological years.

1. TIME & MONEY

The number of times you've circled the sun doesn't tell you how many more there are — or the money needed — to go.

If there is only one solitary number that defines us as human beings, a number that immediately sets us apart from all others – and places our comments in context – it's our age. Speaking formally, age is really nothing more than the sum total of times you have circled the sun, starting with the calendar day on which you were born. And yet that number, more than your height, your width or the circumference of your wallet, positions everything you might do or say in a unique perspective. When we hear a voice or meet someone for the first time, one of the first things we register is their apparent age. We try to guess it. We are often surprised when we learn it. We remain doubtful of it. And, of course, many of us lie about it – perhaps for good and justifiable reasons, as I'll argue in a moment.

Honestly, how seriously do you take comments, suggestions or criticism from a 20-year-old versus a 40-year-old versus a 60-year-old? Age really matters for your pecking order within society. Birthdays are – for most people – the highest personal milestone of the calendar year. It's a date some look forward to with anticipation and others with trepidation, especially as they get older.

For whatever reason, some digits have more meaning than others. Think of the numbers 18, 21, 40, 65 or hitting 100 and becoming a centenarian. These are big deals. Other digits such as 37, 41 or 53 are less noteworthy, as evidenced by the dearth of Hallmark birthday cards with those particular birthdays – I couldn't find any!

This is more than a comment about marketing or psychology. Your legal age is embedded in many aspects of modern life and law. You can't get a driver's license until your age is above Z, you can't purchase alcohol until you are older than X, you can't vote until your age exceeds Y. Age numbers appear in myriads of rules and regulations. And, not surprisingly, every one of these variables can be controversial. Should X, Y and Z be higher? Are they too high? The debate goes on.

Let me get to my point. Although references to age are scattered among all aspects of our highly structured lives, nowhere does this number appear more than in the rules surrounding the arena of retirement planning.

Think of the age at which you can start your government (Social Security) pension, or the age at which you are entitled to tax deductions and credits for being a senior, or the age at which you must start drawing down your retirement account or the age at which you no longer qualify for preferred life insurance. This is more than just about financial regulations. Many jobs, careers and professions force employees to stop working at a fixed age. Think of a highly skilled airline pilot forced to retire at the age 60 (is that fair?) or a government employee who rides off into the sunset at the age of 60 while being paid a sizeable pension (is that fair?)

Within the broad field of retirement planning and investment advising I would argue that age is just as important as that other number: the amount of money you have saved in your nest egg. Your age pops up in all sorts of calculations over your financial and economic lifecycle. Age is used to gauge whether you are saving enough, it dictates a suitable asset allocation or investment portfolio, it determines whether you are spending too much or possibly too little in your senior years. In fact, it wouldn't be an exaggeration to state that no financial conversation about retirement can be conducted these days without age taking center stage. How old are you? And, how much do you have saved? Age is all over your money.

But what if we are using the wrong number?

What if we are calculating age incorrectly? What if the number of years planet earth has circled the sun with you as a passenger is the wrong metric? What if age is like the sand clock on the cover of this book? That is an approximation for true time, developed in the eighth century. Well, if the method for calculating your age is as old as an hourglass, then pension and retirement policy is geared to the wrong number. Large segments of the population are getting a very raw deal.

That is exactly the premise of this book. In fact, I'll argue that the current and common approach to retirement planning – focusing on conventional age, will soon be retired itself. It's on its last breath. What's next, you ask? I say break the glass. Redefine age. Change the clock and replace the dials. I'll get to the details in a moment.

Naturally, if you ask most people to define age, they'll tell you it's simply the difference between today's calendar date and the date on their birth certificate. For example, if today is April 4, 2019 and you were born on April 4, 1967, then you are 52 years old. No subjectivity and no arguments there. Subtracting A from B doesn't require an advanced degree in mathematics. But that is your **chronological** age. The ease of computation is the main reason why this number has become so embedded in our legal life. And, in many cases, it makes perfect sense. It's a great standard which works just fine.

Assume that 16 is the legal age for driving and age 18 for alcohol consumption. I doubt anyone would argue that a child who is a decade younger than the legal limit should be allowed to do either – and especially not at the same time. (In Canada today there's a debate about whether children as young as 16 should be allowed to use cannabis.) On the symmetric other side, if a misguided politician even tried to raise the driving or drinking age by 10 years, they would face a devastating backlash from their constituents – and young kids.

3

Age is obviously a proxy for maturity, physical development, dexterity and perhaps (arguably) rationality. At the age of 16, one rarely looks 15 years older or 15 years younger. Some hit maturity a bit earlier, and some a bit later. There is no big harm in standardizing the driving age at 16, or the voting age or the drinking age.

But let's unpack the chronological age number a bit more and try to understand why it is so critical for *retirement* policy and pension planning.

The age number is most definitely not being used for backward-looking reasons – that is, congratulations, you have been alive for 52 years, you are wise and mature and can operate heavy machinery – but rather *age is being used for its forecasting properties*. When it comes to pensions and retirement, age is not about sexual maturity, emotional intelligence or physical dexterity. Age is actually a proxy for something very different. For what exactly?

Well, whether you like it or not, your age is used to determine how much time you have left. It's meant to measure the distance between you and the Grim Reaper. In retirement planning calculators, formulas, guidelines and regulations, age isn't about measuring the time you have already enjoyed. It's about the time you might have remaining. It's about how many more times you will circle the sun before you leave this earth. Your chronological age is a *proxy* for how many calendar years you have left in your natural life – *and it's a lousy one*.

Table 1.1 illustrates how age is being used. Oh, you are 65? Well, you only have 20 years remaining (on average) so stop working and go enjoy yourself. Congratulations. You are 70 years old? You only have 15 years remaining (on average) and it is time to unlock your tax-sheltered retirement account. You are 80? Well, with five years remaining (on average), we need you to complete much more paperwork before you can buy something, etc. It's all about the number of earth's revolutions around the sun, in the future.

Table 1.1: (Chronological) Age Is All Over Our System	
Age	Legal Implications (in the U.S.)
50.0	Catch-up contributions to 401k/IRA
55.0	No penalty withdrawals from 401k (unemployed)
59.5	Penalty-free withdrawals for 401k (everyone)
60.0	Minimum Social Security (SS) Survivor Benefits
62.0	Minimum Social Security (SS) Retirement Benefits
65.0	Medicare begins & penalty-free HSA withdrawal
67.0	Full (SS) Retirement Age (if born before 1960)
70.0	Maximum Social Security Retirement Benefits
70.5	Required Minimum Distributions from an IRA
85.0	Longevity Annuity Contract (QLAC) must begin
Source: Author compilation	

But What if There Is a Better Way?

Here is my main point. The difference between today's date and the date on your birth certificate does not provide the best indication of how many years you will enjoy in retirement. Note, this isn't a health tip or a factoid that I'm offering here. There are hundreds of billions and possibly trillions of dollars in motion around the world and they all revolve around the definition of age. I'll return to the financial impetus for paying closer attention to age soon enough, but first some science.

There is a growing body of evidence suggesting that an individual's true age can be measured more accurately using *telomeres*, which are protective caps at both ends of your chromosomes. The length of your telomeres provides incremental information superior to other biomarkers of aging. Moreover, the imputed biological age can diverge by as much as 10-20 years from chronological age as measured by calendar years. Now, there are competing methodologies that can be used to measure your biological age and I'll get to those. Telomeres are just the start. Another fertile area revolves around *DNA methylation* and the *epigenetic clock*.

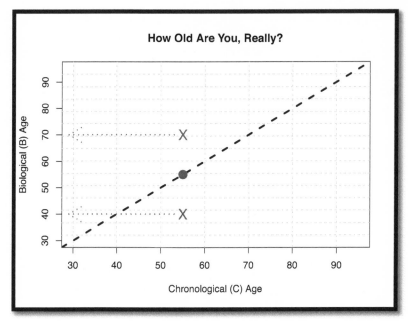

Figure 1.1

My initial point here is that a 55-year-old might in fact be as young as 40 (biologically), or as old as 70 (biologically), when measured properly in terms of forward-looking mortality and morbidity rates. Figure 1.1 offers an early look at this sort of thinking and illustrates the gap between your true (biological) age and your chronological age, although I'm using the word "true" very loosely at this point. So, when you meet a 55-year-old friend or acquaintance you haven't seen for many years and they look much younger, there is a good chance their biological age is in fact 45 or even 40. It's not a mirage. It's biology. They live on the bottom of the diagonal in Figure 1.1.

To be clear, the technology to accurately estimate biological age is still being refined – and other biomarkers of aging might emerge triumphant – and I'll get back to them in chapter #5. But, whether it's telomeres or epigenetic clocks or other molecular markers, good old calendar age is becoming passé.

All this does is raise the possibility that you will soon have access to that number on your phone or watch, *continuously*. There are a number of medical entrepreneurs who are currently working on devices and apps that will take some (minimally invasive) tests and give you a better age, perhaps by averaging the results of all the different numbers being produced by different methods. Standards will materialize and we will eventually look back nostalgically to the days when "age" meant the number of times you circled the sun. Enjoy it while lasts.

Oh, Really?

Well, even if you are skeptical of a consensus emerging about true age, you must acknowledge that this number should be quite relevant to your personal wealth management strategy and retirement income plan. Namely, you must use the right age when deciding how much to save, how much to spend and when to retire. In particular, the widely used and advocated 4% rule of retirement income planning – which you might have heard of – completely ignores aging and longevity and can result in a large disruption in your (or windfall to your heirs) standard of living. As noted above, our entire tax and regulatory system is based on chronological age, independently of your true age, that is your health, life expectancy or mortality prospects. These ages were codified decades ago when life expectancy was much lower – that is a typical 55-year-old's biological age was much higher than it is today. See Table 1.1 again.

Throughout this book I will be arguing that "old" chronological age should take a back seat to "new" biological age in the public discourse around retirement and pension policy. I'll make this case on the grounds of fairness as well as argue that it helps with marketing longevity insurance. Oh yes, I suspect that not all readers will agree, but I do hope you will see why – at the very least – your personal retirement strategy should be calibrated to your biological age and not chronological age. It should be part of the retirement income conversation with your spouse, family, loved ones and/or financial advisor.

Biological Age Thinking

Think about it. Perhaps the earliest age at which you should be entitled to claim your pension should indeed be age 65, but biologically and not chronologically. Consider those who are 70 years old based on calendar time, but are in absolutely perfect health with the physiology of a 50-year-old. Using the language of insurance, their mortality or hazard rate is much lower than an average 70-year-old. Good for them. But should they be entitled to draw a pension for what could be another 40 or 50 years? I don't think so.

On the flip side, imagine those who are 55 years old based on calendar numbers, but for whatever reason – socioeconomic, demographic, racial, etc. – their mortality rate and corresponding life expectancy is much lower than an average 55-year-old. I will provide examples of this later on. This group – and their advocates – have the most to gain from paying attention to this subtle fact. For all intents and purposes these people are 75-year-olds from a biological perspective. Should they have to wait for another 10 to 15 calendar years to draw their pension? Will they ever get there? Is this fair?

Determining Factors

Some might use the less desirable terms like poor health, or sick, or disabled or disadvantaged as the driver of life expectancy. Others will reference race, socioeconomic status, privilege or even good or bad genes. Many will rightfully argue that pension policy should not differentiate or discriminate based on any of these factors. Rather, I would translate all of the emotionally charged language and descriptions into an adjusted age, which I refer to as the *biological age*.

I would suggest that just as a soon as the science is perfected – and the *My-Biological-Age-App* certifies your number – you should be able to draw your pension at a biological age of 65, period. This is regardless of what your driver's license says. That's my policy goal.

Personal Retirement Policy

Now, even if you don't agree with me on the public policy issue – that biological age should replace chronological age – as I wrote earlier, I think you should consider and take account of your own biological age when making retirement and financial decisions. You might not want or think that society's retirement ages and policies should be changed, or that we should redefine age. But how about your own age? Do you ever wonder how old you really are? Did you consider the age at which you should retire? This book can help you on that journey as well.

Figure 1.2 gets to the essence of the personal matter, and at some level is one of the main ideas I would like to impart in this book. It displays a sample path of one of many possible lives. Start at the lower left-hand corner, at the chronological age of 35. Imagine you are in very good relative health, and your biological age (abbreviated B-age) is lower than your C-age and you start your (working) life path *under the diagonal* line. But then, for whatever reason, your relative health starts to deteriorate. Perhaps you neglect yourself, or maybe you have too many sleepless nights (after getting married and caring for young children) and at the chronological age of 45 you find yourself – or your doctor informs you – that you are now *above the diagonal.* Your biological age is 55, which is 10 years above your chronological age. Not good! This information jolts you into action. After improving your diet, exercising regularly, jogging every morning and doing all possible things to improve your health over the next decade, you find yourself (again) under the separating diagonal at the chronological age of 55. Good for you. In fact, under this particular sample path you don't age for the next 10 years, and are still well under the diagonal at the chronological age of 65. But alas, an unexpected devastating jogging accident causes your biological age to jump two decades on a cold, rainy morning. Sadly, you never recover from the accident. It's by (chronological) age 80.

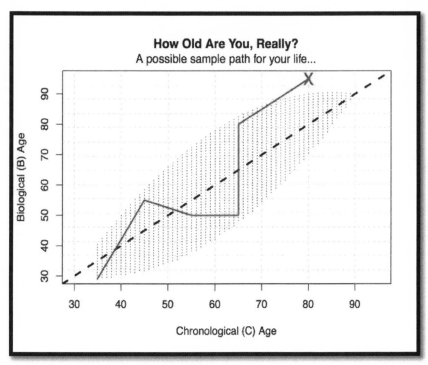

Figure 1.2

Of course, this Figure 1.2 is a realization of just one of the infinitely many sample paths for your biological life (or mortality rate), but hopefully you get the idea. So, where does all of this leave us? Well, regardless of methodology, I do hope this chapter has convinced you – if you weren't already convinced – that your chronological age is, to biological age, what an hourglass is to a Rolex watch. This book will explore the many dimensions and aspects of biological age "thinking" as it relates to insuring and planning your retirement.

Overview of This Book

The ideas in this book are spread across seven related chapters, organized in the following manner.

Chapter #2 goes back a century in time, to when the devastating Spanish influenza virus wreaked havoc on people's health, and indirectly their true age. This was a period when a young parent had the same life expectancy as a retiree and society learned to appreciate the economic value of life insurance protection. It provides me with the opportunity to explain the important pooling mechanism by which insurance operates. The payout money was received by the survivor's family when the breadwinner's longevity was unexpectedly cut short. The insurance company relieved the community and the government from the financial burden of care.

Chapter #3 moves on to a more subtle type of insurance, one that is on the opposite side of dying, namely longevity insurance. This type of protection is embedded in every formal (defined benefit) pension plan, where true age is quite critical in establishing the fairness of the plan. I will argue that as we all learn more about our biological age, collective pension plans that pool individuals based on chronological age will struggle with issues of fairness and equity. Even so, the utility value of longevity insurance is worth it. Pooling risk works both ways.

Chapter #4 discusses the various insurance products or policies that most consumers own, and how longevity insurance can fit into an overall allocation framework. My main point in this chapter is to argue that while readers and commentators might view longevity insurance – such as deferred and immediate income annuities – as a "waste" of money, considering the small chances it will ever get used, their relatively low internal rate of return (IRR) is shared by most insurance policies. It's about protection. In this chapter I also discuss the *longevity insurance* policy that I bought and how it fits into my retirement plan.

Chapter #5 gets to the statistical heart of the matter, focusing on how biological age is measured and how to convert someone's actuarial mortality rate into a true age. It is the most technical part of the book, but key to understanding what I mean by biological age.

Chapter #6 explores another dimension of longevity planning, namely portfolio longevity. It ponders the question: *How old is your nest egg?* It discusses financial products that combine protection against stock market *bears* and longevity *bulls*, all under one umbrella. I make the case for why retirees should think about extending the longevity of their portfolio and insuring against being too young, instead of insuring against becoming a centenarian. This is a matter of positioning and framing, and helps make longevity risk (more) *salient.*

Chapter #7 begins in Russia, then moves on to musings about retirement policy, the implication of modifying the formal definition of age for the purposes of pension eligibility, the ethical implications and closes with a game.

I conclude the book with some heartfelt acknowledgements and provide a list of references with complete citations.

A Note on Sources and References

In an attempt to make this book accessible to as wide an audience as possible, I have refrained from including academic footnotes and citations within the chapter and will make a point of concluding chapters with annotated discussions about further readings.

So, while at times I have made speculative arguments or claims that might sound original to the reader, they can be traced to other (influential) scholars and academics and will be referenced in due time. If you happen to read something and say to yourself "Hey, that was my idea. I published a paper on that back in the stone age," well, there is a good chance the article is referenced at the end of the book.

For example, one of the first economists who advocated adjusting Social Security benefits for (what he labeled) "age inflation" was John Shoven, referenced as (Shoven, 2007) and (Shoven & Goda, 2008).

He credits the economist Victor Fuchs for the original idea, writing in the 1980s, but perhaps it has even earlier providence. Over the years I have found that any good idea can be traced back far enough into the past. It's just a matter of looking.

Not to diminish his contribution, John Shoven makes the great point that a 65-year-old in the year 2000 was equivalent, in terms of mortality rates or remaining life expectancy, to a 59-year-old in the year 1970, hence the term "age inflation." Shoven argues that a retiring male (female) in 2005 was really 7(4) years younger in 2005 versus 1965, which dovetails nicely with my comments about chronological age being rather meaningless. He uses the term *nominal age* versus *real age* to contrast with the equivalent idea of nominal dollars versus real dollars. His main policy point or suggestion is that U.S. social security benefit eligibility ages should be adjusted upwards for *everyone* over time to account for improving health, etc. Shoven wrote, "Pension laws and programs feature lots of conventionally defined ages that haven't changed in 40 years," echoing numbers presented in Table 1.1. He suggested using mortality milestones, say when the mortality rate is 1%, or 5%, to define age, which is related to what I will do in chapter #5.

That said, economists such as Shoven, who have made the inflation argument, haven't focused on age *dispersion*, that is the fact that people with the same chronological age might have very different biological ages. It's unclear they were aware of the extent of the dispersion (or heterogeneity) in ages as per Figures 1.1 or 1.2, when they wrote the article over a decade ago. Nevertheless, I think we all agree that forward-looking remaining life expectancy and not backward-looking calendar years should be the true measure of age. It's nice to have external validation.

Along the same lines, a more recent (academic) article referenced as (Stevens, 2017), discusses a number of different ways in which to adjust government pensions to account for "age inflation," so these are clearly issues that are at the forefront of pension policy.

Needless to say, most people don't think of themselves as being at exactly their chronological age. Some people claim to feel older, and most people claim to feel younger. This has obvious economic implications if people act according to their (rational) beliefs.

For example, an article cited as (Ye & Post, 2018) reports on a survey in which over 12,000 Americans with a typical chronological age of 68 reported feeling 58 years of age, which is a 10-year gap. In other words, *they tend to act how they feel*. So, the concept of not feeling your age isn't new or novel, the question is whether there is any science behind the age you feel, whether that true age should be used for retirement pension policy and how to make sure your money lasts. That's what this book is about.

2. IN FLEW ENZA

Or, how a virus made sudden death salient and legitimized the life insurance industry

To summarize where we are at this point, your true age is *not* necessarily your chronological age, which among many other interesting things implies that your life expectancy – approximately 80 years – might not mean very much either. There is a possibility you might live much longer than 80 calendar years and considerably longer than prior generations. It might be much less than 80 calendar years as well, it all depends on your biological age. As far as retirement planning is concerned, there is quite a bit of uncertainty around the length of time you will be spending (money) in retirement. Nonetheless, there are ways in which to prepare for this randomness, and *longevity insurance* – which I'll explain in much greater detail soon enough – should be a part of your plan and strategy.

Now, for what it's worth, this message has been echoed by many other authors and writers – which I reference and cite in a number of places in this book – and has been at the core of my own research and writing over the last quarter century, as I noted in the prologue. In some sense, readers who stop right here will wonder if there is anything new to say.

Where I depart from the work of others and my own prior writing is by changing the way you think of longevity uncertainty. How long will I live in retirement should be replaced with a more accurate or relevant question:

How old am I?

It's quite clear that an average 70-year-old in the year 2020 is much healthier and in better physical shape than an average 70-year-old was back in the year 1970, which is the cohort born in the year 1900. After all, the current (born in 1950) generation is living relatively longer than the 1900 cohort. Therefore, any pension and retirement policy ages – that were developed in the 1970s – should be adjusted by what economists might call *age inflation*.

Recall that traditional inflation is the process by which the market price of all goods and services increase over time, with some items increasing at a faster rate than others and some items possibly deflating in price. Think of the price of an airline ticket 30 years ago, versus the price of a cup of coffee 30 years ago. One has plummeted, and one has soared. A dollar today is worth much less than a dollar 30 years ago, etc. Well then, age has its own inflation rate as well. Stated tongue in cheek, a 70-year-old today is worth much more than a 70-year-old 70 years ago. I trust you get my point. As I noted at the end of chapter #1, this point has been made by a number of prominent academic economists.

But in addition, I would like to add the concept of *age ambiguity* to the mix. Basically, you don't know how old you really are. Yes, I know. A bit too "new age" for some and this view of the world requires taking a leap of faith. One thing should be clear, as noted in Figure 1.2 in the prior chapter, true age doesn't increase linearly with calendar time. Some individuals will be pleasantly surprised to learn they are younger than their chronological age and others will be alarmed and shocked to hear they might be a decade or two older than the number on their driver's license. Just as we experience different inflation rates depending on how we spend our money, so too we age at different rates.

Where Are We Going with This?

Moving forward, your concept of age should be adjusted for two things: (i) age *inflation* over time, and (ii) age inflation *heterogeneity* across different segments of the population. Both of these adjustments in thinking take time to absorb and implement because these shocks aren't visible or readily observed with precision over short periods of time. Hyperinflation in countries like Venezuela or Zimbabwe is easily observable and quite salient. The effect of a meager 2% inflation rate, which has been experienced in North America over the last few decades, is much harder to observe or appreciate. It isn't very salient.

In fact, changes in human life expectancy and mortality improvements aren't really shocks in the true sense of the word, but slow realizations that accumulate over long periods of time. Humans often struggle to adapt to these sorts of gradual changes. Every new cohort that is born appears to live just a few more months than the prior cohort. Is this a big deal?

Indeed, you never hear of the opposite, that is hyperdeflation, where prices of all goods and services plummet overnight. What is more common is hyperinflation, where prices jump, but both moves would be damaging. Not unlike inflation, nature's sudden longevity shocks only occur in one direction – that is a negative one – and it really has been almost a full century since the world has experienced its last longevity shock.

Most readers have forgotten (or never knew) about this shock to begin with, but a shock it was. I would suggest it's helpful to review the details of this last jolt to mortality rates and specifically to examine how the financial industry coped with that episode. It has lessons to impart in a Biological Age and era.

For readers who haven't figured it out by now, the shock I am referring to is the 1918 influenza pandemic, a.k.a. the Spanish flu, also nicknamed the Spanish Lady, which killed somewhere between 50 million and possibly as many as 100 million people around the world. In the next few pages I'll provide a high-level summary, discuss the so-called shocking aspects of this flu – which isn't what you might expect – and then move on to how the financial and insurance industries coped. It's at the heart and foundation of risk pooling, which is quite important for understanding how to mitigate longevity risk as well.

The Spanish Flu

Slightly over a century ago, in January 1918, doctors at a military camp in Haskell County, Kansas, USA, were puzzled by cases of local soldiers with severe flu symptoms. In the most extreme cases the signs of severe illness included hemorrhaging (i.e. massive bleeding) from the nose, ears and stomach. A painful and rapid death followed the symptoms with a very high probability, with the official cause of death being pneumonia or massive hemorrhaging itself.

At first – what much later became known as the Spanish flu – the illness was misdiagnosed by observers as cholera or even typhoid, both of which have similar symptoms. But, by early March 1918, American doctors and pathologists realized they were dealing with a very different beast. By then it had mushroomed into a global monstrosity that spread via sneezing and coughing, by tiny and very deadly virus particles. Table 2.1 displays what you need to know about the Spanish flu.

The precise origin or patient zero of the Spanish flu pandemic is controversial (note: a pandemic is an epidemic that has spread around the world). Some claim that it originated in other locations within the U.S. in mid-1917, and other researchers argue that the flu originated in East Asia and in particular China. I'll refer interested readers to the (ever-changing, somewhat unreliable, reviled) *Wikipedia* page, in addition to some more respectable references with sources on the latest volley in an ongoing debate about the cause of the virus. What isn't in dispute is that (i) it originated in ducks and pigs and then jumped to humans, (ii) it is a strain of the H1N1 virus and, most importantly, (iii) it spread around the world by soldiers engaged in the conflict of World War I.

Recall that in early 1918 – that is before the famous Armistice Day of November 11, 1918 – the world was deep in the fog of battle, with troops moving around Europe and living in close quarters within the theatre of war. All of this created a fertile breeding ground for the Spanish flu virus, which marched around the globe from one pliable host to another with remarkable speed. Needless to say, antibiotics had not yet been developed and commercialized, but even if they had been, they could not have stopped the virus.

Ironically, in the year 1918, the war effort itself spread the virus but also obscured or shrouded it. Many countries in Europe as well as the U.S. were rightfully hesitant to allow open reporting of the new and deadly flu – for fear it would impact the troops' morale – and used the war censorship process to conceal the extent of the pandemic. Media reports among both the Allied and Central powers, were limited and tame. The newspapers were devoid of the (scary) headlines one might have expected from a salacious press. Compare this to the headlines during the bird flu in the 1990s or the SARS scare during the early years of the 21st century. As far as the government was concerned, officially speaking, if people (soldiers) were dying from an unknown illness, battles and fighting were officially to blame.

This also helps explain the Spanish origins for the name of the flu. The country of Spain was one of the few neutral countries (in addition to the Scandinavian countries) during the war, so the Spanish media were free to report on anything they liked, including the new and deadly flu making its way around the world. Alas, when Spain's reigning king Alfonso XIII was infected (in the spring 1918) with the flu (for a second time, actually) and suffered the above-noted symptoms, the world's media included regular updates on his status. So, as far as history is concerned, the pandemic will always be associated with Spain (although in Spain the virus was nicknamed the Naples Soldier).

For the record, King Alfonso XIII survived the 1918 flu and recovered fully despite the ruthless odds. But history wasn't kind to him. A mere 10 years later he was accused of high treason by his countrymen and he fled the country in disgrace in 1930, settling in

Rome. He then abdicated the throne and died (peacefully) in 1941, more than two decades after recovering from a bad case of the flu. He will be known (in infamy) as the person who bequeathed the name Spanish flu to the world, as well as indirectly spawning the cruelties of the Spanish civil war and General Francisco Franco.

Table 2.1: Facts About the Spanish Influenza Pandemic	
Time Period (over 3 waves)	March 1918 to May 1919
Global Infection Rate	1/3 of World Population
Mortality Rate (if infected)	Between 10% and 20%
Global Death Toll	Min: 50 to Max: 100 million
Mortality Extremes	Iran (20%) vs. Japan (0.5%)
American & Canadians	725,000 deaths
Likely Cause of Death	Pneumonia (cytokine storm)
Source: See reference section	

World War I, which technically ended with the Treaty of Versailles in June 1919, killed approximately 17 million people. In contrast to the death toll from this human-made conflict, the Spanish flu surrendered after having killed at least 50 million people around the world, and possibly even double that number.

Now, the large margin of error (tens of millions) in estimating the death toll is unfathomable in today's world, but one must remember and be cognizant of the difficulties in properly accounting for a cause of death – or even identifying a death – during such a turbulent period. One thing is for certain, the Spanish flu was deadlier than World War I, although with fewer memorials, statues or statutory holidays. History books might have forgotten the details, but at the time of the outbreak, the American public was well aware of the war with germs (as well as Germans) and took precautions.

For the record, October 1918 was the worst month, and churches, schools and theatres were closed. Victory parades were mostly outlawed, but bars and taverns remained open as long as patrons took the bottled beer home with them to drink in private.

Face masks were enforced in public, mainly to prevent the estimated 40,000 droplets that were released every time someone sneezed from infecting others. In fact, New York City passed an ordinance imposing jail time and fines for people who didn't cover their mouths when they coughed. (Perhaps that's an ordinance that should be resurrected.)

From Morbidity to Mortality

Approximately one-third of the world's population was infected (morbidity) and became ill during the influenza pandemic. That is, approximately 500 million people became ill around the world. From that large unlucky group, 10% to as many as 20% died from causes related to the virus, leading to a mortality rate of between 3% and 6% globally, according to estimates made in the 1970s. More recently, the Centers for Disease Control (CDC) in Atlanta estimated that the (unconditional) mortality rate from the Spanish flu was 2.5% globally, which is slightly lower than the 6% figure suggested above. The extra deaths, they claim, were attributed to World War I, not the flu. Anyway, the debate goes on. These are broad brushstrokes. Some countries and regions were affected much worse than others. See comparisons for Iran and Japan, for example, in Table 2.1

Closer to home, 675,000 Americans (from a population of approximately 105 million) and 50,000 Canadians (from a population of approximately 8.5 million) died from the flu during an approximate 18-month period. The implied mortality rates in North America, which were approximately 0.6% for both Canadians and Americans, were lower than the global mortality rates. These rates are consistent with the fact that North America suffered relatively less from the Spanish flu compared to other regions, such as Europe and Asia.

Getting back to the topic of variability, Iran lost 22% of its population to the Spanish flu, while Brazil's isolated communities in the Amazon delta weren't affected. The reasons for these regional variations in mortality rates are still being debated a century later.

For example, the governor of American Samoa imposed a strict quarantine on the island, which explains the reduced infection rate to virtually nil. Yet another possible explanation for the variation in mortality rates across countries is the age distribution of the population, which brings me to my next point – and perhaps a shocking one.

The Longevity Shock

Separate and distinct from the variation in mortality, was how the mortality rates varied as a function of the afflicted person's chronological age. In particular, what was completely unexpected at the time was the age distribution of *who* was infected and *who* died. This gets to the essence of the longevity shock I mentioned earlier. Normally one might expect that older, naturally frail and weak people would be the most vulnerable to such a pandemic, with a higher propensity for infection and death. But the reality was surprisingly quite different.

First, 99% of the deaths in the U.S. from the Spanish flu were individuals *under* the age of 65, and half of the deaths from the flu were young and middle-aged people between the ages of 20 and 40. One might say the virus preyed on the strong and energetic, while the naturally weak and diminished survived.

This was – and continues to be – quite mystifying for epidemiologists who study (and puzzle over) these matters. But it's more than just young versus old. Figure 2.1 displays the mortality or death rate from the Spanish flu as a function of age, with a noticeable spike around the age of 28. It's quite a jarring picture and should elicit a wow moment. It did for me. This is what I refer to as "the longevity shock."

Going back to the concept of biological versus chronological age, looking at this figure it seems that during the period of the Spanish flu, although your chronological age might have been 28, your biological age was 75. The mortality rate was the same! *But why?*

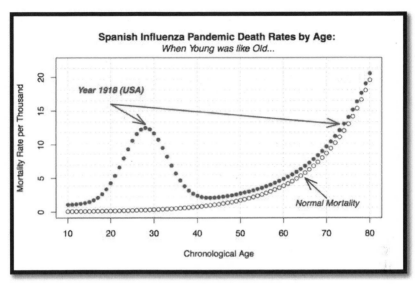

Figure 2.1

Well, if you think of biological age as being closely associated with mortality rates, and rates between 20 and 40 spiked, then your biological age spiked as well. Suddenly, overnight, you aged by 20 to 40 years as measured by your life expectancy. I'll discuss mortality rates in much greater detail in chapter #5, but researchers have estimated that life expectancy dropped by 12 full years due to this spike in mortality. The equivalent of hyperinflation for mortality. And again, it was the youngest (chronologically) adults who experienced the highest death rate.

Now, like many other aspects of the Spanish flu narrative, the reasons for this puzzlingly low mortality rate among the elderly, has been subject to much scientific speculation. Some have conjectured that older adults might have developed an immunity of sorts because they would have been alive and exposed to a pandemic 30 years earlier in the 1890s (known as the Russian flu). Others have suggested gender stereotypes as a factor. Supposedly, "real men" didn't need to rest when they were infected with the flu – something they obviously did require in hindsight – which ended up killing them with greater frequency, relative to those who took time off and went to bed. But there was obviously more to it than lack of rest.

The younger (and stronger) the biological immune system, the harder it was to fight off the Spanish flu. The more an individual was willing and able to fight the disease, the more it fought back. And, it usually won. I would call it the 20th century's first and greatest longevity shock.

Here is just one interesting anecdote about what this Spanish Lady did to many young strong American (and actually Canadian) men. The only time in history that the Stanley Cup hockey finals ever had to be canceled was in 1919, during the third and final wave of the Spanish flu, which hit in the spring of that year. Even during years of war, the famed hockey league managed to cobble together enough reserve players – the real teams had volunteered and went off to fight – and managed to complete a full season. But in the spring of 1919 the final series was canceled when most of the Montreal Canadiens (a perennial favorite at the time, because they had won the most games) were bedridden. After five games the championship was cancelled. One is hard pressed to think of a group of people who are more suited to fight a disease or war, on or off the ice.

Enter Life Insurance

Now, some readers might find it callous of me to focus on (hockey or) the rather trivial aspects of money in the wake of what has been described as the greatest *medical* holocaust in history, but the insurance industry is quite central to the story here. For all intents and purposes, insurance companies were the only ones that could protect families against the financial consequences of this longevity shock. By pooling small amounts of money from large groups of policyholders who paid regular periodic premiums, the companies were able to create a very large fund that could be used to support and pay the beneficiaries. For example, 10,000 people might pay an insurance premium of $100, creating a pool of $1 million. And, if

1% of the pool died, each beneficiary would receive 1% of the pool, that is a $10,000 death benefit. They paid $100 and received $10,000. It might seem to be magic, or perhaps a *ponzi* scheme, to those who aren't familiar with the principle of insurance. That's the essence of risk pooling.

As noted earlier, one quarter of the U.S. population was infected by the Spanish flu, and although most recovered, an average of 1,250 Americans died every single day over a period of 18 months, leading to a loss of 675,000 lives.

Many – although certainly not all – of those who died owned life insurance policies, which committed the insurance company to pay the beneficiaries hundreds of thousands of dollars. Although it was unclear at the time whether these insurance companies could sustain such financial pressure and survive the flu themselves.

Not unlike many other industries in the economy, insurance companies lost employees (and executives) and obviously had a difficult time maintaining day-to-day operations. A beneficiary couldn't receive a death benefit payout or check if the agent himself – and perhaps his entire back office – was infected with or died of the flu.

Some agents (who weren't infected) reported issuing or selling a policy to a family one week, barely having collected only one single premium payment, only to return the next week to pay the family because the insured, perhaps a parent or father, had died. The *National Underwriter* (a popular industry magazine) wrote the following on January 16, 1919. It was still in the midst of the flu, but a few months after the worst had passed. "Almost all agents have had startling experiences during the last few months of soliciting people for insurance, who in a few days were stricken with the flu and died." Kudos. I suspect that if this happened today, a death so soon after the policy was issued, the claim would be challenged or disputed by the company. Ah, the good old days.

Back to pooling again, as I explained with my simple example, the only way the principle or model of life insurance works is if many people pay small premiums to the insurance company over long periods of time – and don't die quickly – so that the company has enough reserves to pay the few who perish along the way. The essence of risk pooling – which I'll return to again, in the context of pensions and longevity insurance in the next chapter – is the risk of having many people buying insurance who never make a claim or do so very far into the future. Could the insurance industry cope?

<u>Marketing Bonanza</u>

Well, the insurance companies survived, and they thrived. I would argue – and I don't say this lightly – that the Spanish flu was one of the best things that happened to the insurance industry (at least in the U.S.) in the early part of the 20th century. This might sound quite odd, crass and perhaps even cruel, but it's true. The flu and its aftermath was a godsend to anyone whose business it was to *sell* life insurance.

According to estimates published in the 1920s in the same *National Underwriter* – a publication which actually survives to this day, by the way – the insurance industry paid out claims totaling 0.5% of the U.S. GDP as a result of the Spanish flu. In today's dollars that sum would be approximately $30 billion. This can be compared to (approximately) $80 billion that the insurance industry paid out in the year 2018, for example. When you consider this was paid out a century ago, it's an astonishing sum of money.

Don't get me wrong. It was a scary and stressful time for the industry. Some insurance companies (mutual companies, really) had to suspend dividends to shareholders and policy holders. Others required emergency loans from banks to help with liquidity constraints and the inability to sell investments. In fact, there were cases of insurance company checks that should have bounced due to insufficient funds in the relevant accounts, but there were stories of heroic and trusting bank managers who honored the payments, knowing that eventually the company would cover the IOUs.

Back to the pool once more, from a financial risk management perspective, insurance companies had marked up or loaded their insurance premiums by a sufficient margin to (just barely) cover such a statistical anomaly. For some companies that were particularly hard hit, the actual number of claims exceeded the expected number of claims by up to 50%. In other words, they hadn't really charged enough in premiums to cover the risk, but those were rare cases and overall companies had enough reserves to cover payouts. I'll say that the industry's survival (from the Spanish flu) was a success story for actuarial science. Here is the bottom economic line: The insurance companies charged enough and held enough in reserves to pay claims. Yes, there were some eventual insolvencies and bankruptcies a few years later, but many of those can be blamed on the Great Depression or other isolated calamities before and after 1918.

But here is an important point. The reason the Spanish flu was (somewhat of) a godsend for the insurance industry gets back to the issue of who exactly died. Recall that the 28-year-old men in Figure 2.1 were also most likely to be new parents themselves with young children at home. These men were likely to have been breadwinners and their deaths likely resulted in their families being left penniless and indigent.

Those families fortunate enough to own and have life insurance – a practice not yet widespread by any means – meant they had some measure of financial security. But those who died without owning life insurance, whether out of negligence or for reasons of faith, left families destitute at the mercy of the community and society. Remember, this was decades before (the old New Deal) what today is called Social Security in the U.S.

Alas, with the heartbreaking tragedy that was experienced all over the U.S., there were financial winners and financial losers. The two distinct groups were quite visible, vocal and rather perversely served as a brilliant advertisement for the benefits of life insurance.

The Spanish flu made mortality risk and life insurance *salient*. Salient is defined as being notable, conspicuous and standing out. When our attention is drawn to a particular fact or specific item, set against a larger background of noise and distraction, it becomes salient. People noticed the widespread randomness and counter-intuitive mortality rate from the Spanish flu. The risk of an early death became a real possibility, and life insurance was an effective way of protecting against this risk.

According to the *National Underwriter*, one of the first questions that onlookers would ask at funerals or upon hearing of another tragic death of a young breadwinner was: "Did they have life insurance?" It would be the only solace for a community that was reeling from many other deaths and the financial burdens these imposed.

Later, in the 1920s, the insurance industry went even one step further and created advertisements in magazines and newspapers that capitalized on (or some might say took advantage of) the Spanish flu. Marketing departments and executives leveraged the sudden salience of risk – which did not last very long thanks to fading memories – to promote life insurance, a product that previously had not garnered much respect.

As an example, the Massachusetts Mutual Life Insurance Company, which is still around today by the way, ran a big advertisement for its life insurance products in the *New York Times*. The full-page ad was ominous sounding with its emphasis on "sudden": "Spanish Influenza: Can You Afford Sudden Death?" I presume most people could only afford the *gradual* kind of death. But in their defense, the insurance industry wasn't the only group taking advantage of the nascent *salience* of the Spanish flu to flog commercial and industrial products. Local drug stores and even pharmacists did the same by promoting regular doses of "flaxseed oil as an antidote to the flu." These advertisements were just as garish. (P.S. Flaxseed oil doesn't really do any good.)

Bad Reputation Repaired

The insurance industry had an appalling image in the decade or two before the Spanish flu pandemic, and some might argue it still does. But I can tell you, its reputation was worse then. At the time, its bad reputation was partly because the industry was deeply involved in scandals relating to the sale of (something called) *tontine insurance* policies. As a result, a substantial segment of the population believed life insurance was a form of gambling, unethical and corrupt. Some argued that sales of something that only pays if you die should be banned on moral grounds, even though many of the policies acted like personal pensions and savings plans. Remember, this was before the Social Security program.

To be crystal clear, people died before the Spanish flu and obviously continued to die after the Spanish flu. Many had life insurance. In fact, approximately 120,000 Americans died in the violence and battles of World War I, most of which were unrelated to the flu. But, high mortality death rates from war were expected and the military cared for its own. Likewise, old people died and some owned life insurance policies, but the financial benefit to the family wasn't immediate. After all, when a 70-year-old died and a 40-year-old or 50-year-old descendant received a windfall settlement, the societal benefits weren't as clear.

However, when a 28-year-old-old father (or pregnant mother) died from the Spanish flu, the young family received an immediate and substantial financial disbursement. In this scenario, the social benefits were clear and evident to all. It was one family that wouldn't have to rely on public (or church) charity. Life insurance products thus gained broad social utility and respectability during the 1920s and 1930s. Nobody questioned the need for, or value of, life insurance when it immediately and evidently relieved the burden of care from the community and extended family. From the 1920s onward, the insurance industry earned a stature and power that persists a full century later. The days of scandal are long gone.

A full century later whenever some enterprising politician or lawmaker threatens to tinker with any of the tax or regulatory benefits enjoyed by the insurance industry, the retort and defense of the status quo inevitably revolves around references to widows and orphans that will be left destitute. This is marketing material straight from the 1920s.

The Spanish flu not only made the death of a breadwinner salient, it also legitimized its economic and financial antidote: life insurance. In some sense, one needs the same sort of shock for longevity risk. Perhaps the industry needs the same kind of (garish) advertisement promoting longevity insurance and the need for lifetime income every time someone hits the age of 100. At every advanced birthday, people should be asking, "Does he have longevity insurance?"

The Spanish flu pandemic is a great example of risk salience leading to increased life and health insurance purchases. There are other examples in the property and casualty arena – a sudden rush to buy insurance – but only after natural disasters such as hurricanes, floods and fires. The San Francisco earthquake and subsequent fire of 1906, which destroyed most of the city and has been compared to the Spanish flu as a similar case study in disaster management, had the same effect. It made these risks salient and increased the interest in and demand for protection. The tendency of consumers to disproportionately weigh recent risk can be manipulated by the industry to sell unnecessary and financially useless products, but that takes us far beyond the agenda for this book. The next logical step, and the next chapter in fact, will dig deeper into this concept of longevity insurance and how it actually works.

Sources and References

The Spanish flu is a fertile area of research for historians, biologists, epidemiologists and even economists. For example, an article in the *Journal of Political Economy*, cited as (Almond, 2006), purports to show that cohorts *in utero* during the pandemic experienced reduced educational attainment, increased rates of physical disability, lower income and lower socioeconomic status well into their retirement years, compared with birth cohorts on either side of 1918. In other words, their economic prospects were worse. The effects of the pandemic weren't transient by any means.

In the lead up to and the marking of the centennial year of the pandemic, there has been a resurgence of interest in a period of history that didn't receive as much attention as it deserved a hundred years ago.

Two recent books I found interesting are cited as (Barry, 2009) and (Arnold, 2018). Although the focus of each book is quite different, and the book by John Barry was originally published in 2004, both books were profiled quite favorably in the *Wall Street Journal* in early 2018.

The Economist magazine published a long article (in the September 29, 2018 issue) on the pandemic, as did Tristin Hopper in the (Canadian) *National Post*, where I learned about the one (1919) year in which the Stanley Cup wasn't awarded. The American Council of Life Insurance (www.ACLI.com) posted a number of data-driven pieces on the pandemic, extolling the insurance industry's ability to survive the pandemic. A particularly good series of articles was published by Allison Bell in www.ThinkAdvisor.com, leading up to the centennial year, which is a source for some of the anecdotes in this chapter. In 2013 the consulting firm *AIR Worldwide* estimated that a similar disaster today would cost U.S. life insurers $28 billion. All of these articles (and many more) can be located with a simple Google search.

For readers intrigued by the mortality peak around age 28, or the implications that a 28-year-old had the same life expectancy as a 70-year-old – see the article cited as (Gagnon, et al., 2013). They theorize that early exposure to the Russian (1889) flu pandemic, or what they called a "dysregulated immune response," killed them.

Another interesting theory is that Germany went from imminent victor, in the fall of 1918, to retreat and defeat, due to the havoc caused by the Spanish flu. Intriguing, but ultimately speculative. See the *Encyclopedia of the First World War*, for more.

Finally and more generally, with regards to the idea that pandemics such as the Spanish flu helped – and are possibly manipulated by – the insurance industry in advertising campaigns, see the excellent book cited as (Gardner, 2008).

3. PENSION ECONOMICS

---

*Where you will learn of winners and losers in the game of
pensions, but why it still pays to play in a younger crowd.*

At this juncture I presume you appreciate or "get" the benefits of
life insurance, as well as the economic concept of a large group of
people pooling small amounts to help pay the beneficiaries of those
who die. Another take-away from chapter #2 is that "the longevity
shock" of the 1918 Spanish influenza pandemic helped solidify life
insurance as a reputable and essential risk management instrument
for all young families. It furnished the product with a respectable
veneer, versus a crass gamble or bet against fate on how long one
might live. The pandemic's random and unexpected deaths
(especially at age 28) helped make the risk *salient*. This is why a
century later it's hard to find any financial commentators who
dispute the importance and need for pure life insurance. It's the
backbone of a personal financial strategy and sound risk-
management plan for the family. If there is any debate really, it's
around how much protection a family should have (5 times salary?
10 times salary?) and which type to use (whole life insurance, term
insurance, universal?). But the need is indisputable. Even the most
investment-oriented of financial advisors or planners would never
attempt to compute the internal rate of return (IRR) on a simple life
insurance policy and argue that it wasn't as high or as good as the
long-term return from a low-cost mutual fund or ETF (exchange
traded fund.) An investment fund can't replicate or beat home
insurance, car insurance, disability insurance or life insurance. So you
can't use investment metrics to analyze their value.

My objective in this chapter is to focus on the symmetric opposite
of life insurance that pays beneficiaries upon death of the insured –
that is, longevity insurance that pays for living (more) and not dying
(young).

Now, for those readers who are getting used to the idea of insurance in case *you live a long time*, it might sound like an odd type of insurance, but in fact it's more common than you think. It's actually embedded inside your retirement (Social Security) pension benefits, so everyone (and I mean everyone) already has some of this insurance. But I think they need more, which I'll get to soon enough.

Needless to say, the longevity risk against which it protects isn't as salient as death, and very often gets ignored all together in the discussion of pension plans and types. In fact, one of the (many) growing challenges with traditional (defined benefit) pensions is that the insurance benefit isn't evenly distributed across all the participants who are pooled together, often resulting in winners and losers. This, then, touches upon the heart of one of the ideas in this book, namely that pension eligibility should be based on true biological age and not chronological age, but I am getting ahead of myself.

What Does a Pension Annuity Do?

First, to understand the nature of pooling within pension plans – in contrast to the very obvious and intuitive mechanics of a life insurance policy – I'll begin with a simple example that will form the narrative backbone of this chapter and the ones to follow.

Assume that Mrs. Heather is about to retire at the (chronological) age of 65 and is entitled to a pension annuity, that is, Social Security, or guaranteed income of exactly $25,000 per year, paid monthly for the remainder of her life. This is the maximum she can receive from her scheme after having worked the requisite number of years. Lucky for her the pension annuity payments are adjusted or increased every year for the cost of living or price inflation as measured by some national index. However, the income will cease upon her death. It contains no cash value or liquidity provisions, nor can she bequeath the pension income to her children, grandchildren or loved ones.

Note here that I'm not describing any one specific country or government plan, but rather a generic no frills defined benefit (DB) pension scheme managed by any large sponsor. Needless to mention, your pension scheme – if you are lucky to be a member of one – might have some different features, guarantees or provisions. At this point I would like to focus on the big picture and on how to "think" about having an income for life.

Now, coincidentally, her nextdoor neighbor Mr. Simon Black, who was born in the same year as Mrs. Heather, is also about to retire at age 65 and is entitled to the same pension annuity of $25,000 per year. He too has contributed the maximum to the pension scheme or retirement program, perhaps explicitly by having a fraction of his paycheck withheld or implicitly via the income tax system. The details of how Simon and Heather paid for the entitlement to their pension annuity are unimportant at this juncture. The key element, though, is that over his working life Simon has contributed the same amount of money as Heather to the pension system. My *all-else-being-equal* story might sound like an attempt to thread a proverbial camel through the eye of a needle, but for now it's all hypothetical and allows me to create identical working lives for both Simon and Heather.

We now get to the (biological) heart of the matter. There is one important difference between Simon and Heather, though. Regrettably, Simon has a medical life expectancy of 10 years and is rather sickly, whereas Heather is in perfect health with a corresponding life expectancy of 30 years – and they both know it.

How do they know? Assume they have both subjected themselves to one of the many genetic tests that measure their pre-disposition to life shortening diseases, or have had their telomeres measured (which I mentioned in chapter #1). Perhaps they were scanned using other biomarkers of aging, such as DNA methylation. I'll discuss procedures in more detail when I get to the measuring of true age in chapter #5. Either way, they have both undergone a rigorous medical examination and their disparate life expectancy verdicts (10 vs. 30) are the consensus opinion of medical experts. Heather will live to age 95 (from the current age of 65) and outlive Simon by 20 years, who will only make it to 75. Or, stated using the language that permeates most of this book, although their chronological ages are both 65, Heather's biological age is much lower than Simon's biological age.

And yet, despite Simon's poor health – and the financial fact he contributed the exact same amount to the retirement program – he isn't entitled to any more income from his pension annuity compared to Heather. In the language of insurance, retirement programs aren't underwritten or adjusted for individual health status. In fact, most government Social Security programs around the world are unisex as well as gender neutral. If you contributed (the maximum amount) into the system, you will receive the same benefit regardless of your sex or health status or the amount of time you are expected to live in retirement. Under the banner of social solidarity, and for better or worse, the Simons and Heathers of the world are all in the same retirement program together.

Now you might *believe* this is completely normal, fair and socially progressive and that any pension scheme should not discriminate in any way – and I have no intention of arguing with you. Rather, I would like to focus attention on the financial implications of this blindness towards gender, health, demographics and genetic predisposition. Who wins and who loses when they are all pooled together? By how much?

It's quite clear that Simon's short life expectancy of 10 years implies that he will be receiving (much) less income compared to Heather. Moreover, if the retirement program is designed to neither make nor lose money in the long-run, that is, be actuarially balanced, then the (sick) Simons of the world are subsidizing the (healthy) Heathers.

Once again, this statement isn't meant to be controversial or debatable. It's the exact opposite of life insurance. In this case, people who die early, or young, subsidize those who live a long and healthy life. If the wealth transfer does come up in polite conversation, the justification provided for the subsidy is that notwithstanding the current unfairness, it might be desirable to help undo or repair historical inequities. Alas, that is the nature of all social programs and other public policies designed to provide assistance. Others will argue in defense of this demographic blindness that in practice most real-world Heathers are entitled to only $15,000 (not $25,000) per year while most real-world Simons are receiving $30,000 (not $25,000) in pension income. Indeed, perhaps Heather was forced to leave work and the labor force over multiple years to give birth, raise a family or take care of an infirm relative. In other words, the transfer isn't that large.

Again, I'm not arguing the transfer is unfair or unprecedented. Most income tax systems are progressive, which means that high-income taxpayers subsidize low-income taxpayers. But in this case, the transfer is from those with shorter lives to those with longer lives. Once again there is no absence of loud, emotional and historical explanations offered to justify why Simon's pension annuity should be the exact same as Heather's and that her obviously longer life expectancy shouldn't affect her entitlements. In fact, today in most of Europe, insurance companies are prohibited from using gender to price *any* type of insurance policy, whether it be life, health, home or even car insurance.

My intent here isn't to argue against the subsidy. Rather, what I would like to do in the next few pages is develop a framework to help quantify the magnitude of the subsidy from Simon to Heather and illustrate that it's quite large under reasonable parameters. And yet, at the same time, *I'll argue that Simon still benefits from being a member of this pension scheme because it pools people together and provides longevity insurance.* In fact Simon's longevity risk is greater than Heather's, even if he isn't expected to live as long. More on that to come.

It all might sound rather paradoxical at first and I'll obviously elaborate. In fact, I will do so using recently available demographic data on the magnitude of longevity risk and how it varies by income and nationality. Finally, getting back to the main undercurrent and theme of this book in chapter #7, I'll argue that although Simon benefits from longevity risk pooling under the current system, it could be made even better and fairer by allowing Heather and Simon to retire at a biological age of 65 (for example) instead of the chronological age of 65. The question of how exactly to measure biological age will be addressed in chapter #5, once I provide more information on the pension motivation and the nature of pooling that is embedded inside every longevity insurance policy.

Pricing Life & Annuities

To get to the essence of the pooling and subsidies from a financial perspective, the next issue I address is as follows: How much would Simon have to pay in the open (i.e. retail) market to acquire a pension annuity of $25,000 per year? How much would Heather have to pay? You might think that only pension plans can offer these annuities, but they are in fact available for purchase from most private life insurance companies, no different than private life insurance. Elsewhere I have referred to this process as *pensionizing your nest egg*. That price or cost should give a rough sense of the magnitude of the transfer provided by Simon to Heather.

Now, in practice, the market price would depend on many factors, including the uncertainty around Simon's and Heather's life expectancy. So, to keep things very simple (at first), I'll assume that Simon will live for exactly 10 years longer and Heather will live for exactly 30 years longer. In other words, I'll assume it's not an average but a reality. And, for the actuarial and insurance readers who are unhappy with this assumption, perhaps I can assuage your concerns by assuming the pension annuity is a "term- certain annuity" and will only pay Simon for 10 years and Heather for 30 years.

Either way, here are the financial facts of life. Simon would be charged $212,750 at the chronological age of 65 and Heather would be charged $487,250 for the same exact pension annuity. These numbers are based on a 3% effective (real) annual interest rate, no default risk and ignoring taxes, but does not require much else in terms of assumptions or parameters.

Stated differently, the present value of $25,000 per year for 10 years is exactly $212,750. But for 30 years of cash flow the present value is $487,250. And, thinking in terms of a collective pool, the market cost of their combined pension annuity entitlement is $212,750 + $487,250 = $700,000. So, if – and this is a big if – the scheme is properly funded (i.e. actuarially balanced), it should have exactly $700,000 set aside in reserves to pay pension annuities for Heather and Simon at the exact point or moment of retirement.

Okay. Spoiler alert here: Very few pension schemes have anywhere near the $700,000 set aside that is needed to pay all the guaranteed pension annuities, which is yet another reason for reform. But I'm getting way ahead of myself here and it's not relevant to the economic value of Heather's and Simon's pension entitlement. Proper funding of government and state pensions is more of a political issue really, and far outside the mandate of this book.

To be clear, real-world insurance companies will not charge $212,750 and $487,250 to Simon or Heather for true life annuities. First and foremost, these companies have to make profits, so they would mark up or load the price no different than the retail versus the wholesale cost of coffee. More importantly, insurance companies have to budget and provision for uncertainty, including the risk of how long their annuitants will live. I'll get to all that later on. There is no point jumping to the graduate course on Actuarial Science 201 before we settle the basics of Financial Economics 101.

The first take away from these two numbers is as follows: Simon is transferring $137,250 to Heather. This is a subsidy amounting to 64.5% of the hypothetical value of Simon's pot of money. Why? Again, the pension system should have $750,000 set aside for both of them, of which $487,250 is needed for Heather and only $212,750 is needed for Simon. And yet, they both contributed the same amount of money to the system – presumably a total of $350,000 x 2 = $700,000 over the course of their working life. Simon contributed $350,000 and is getting something worth $137,250 less. Heather contributed $350,000 and is getting something worth $137,250 more, namely the market price of the pension annuity she will receive for the rest of her life. Table 3.1 provides a summary.

Table 3.1: The Value of Your Pension Entitlement		
	Simon 65	Heather 65
Annuity Income	$25,000 p.a.	$25,000 p.a.
Life Horizon	10 years	30 years
Annuity Value (A)	$212,750	$487,250
Contributions (B)	$350,000	$350,000
Transfer A – B	-$137,250	+$137,250
Subsidy (A – B) / A	-64.5%	+28.2%
Source: Author calculations		

Yes, of course, these are straw men and women. The numbers assume a pension system with no spousal or survivor benefits and a (somewhat extreme) 20-year gap in life expectancy between the two. More importantly, my simple tale assumes that Simon and Heather die precisely at their life expectancy, which presumes the absence of any longevity risk or uncertainty. In reality, Simon might live beyond age 75 (or he may die even earlier), and Heather might not make it to age 95 (or she may live even longer). Under those outcomes the subsidy might be smaller (or even larger.)

We really won't know precisely *who paid whom* until they both pass away, or as economists would say, *ex post*. But the *ex ante* reality is that there is a large gap between the expected present value of the benefits they receive even though they have paid similar amounts into the retirement program. In fact, if there are more Heathers than Simons in the program, the subsidy provided by Simon is even greater. Vice versa, if the retirement program is stacked with many more Simons relative to fewer Heathers, the subsidy provided by any one Simon isn't as large and might yet be another reason for why this issue isn't a big deal.

To make this point, for example, using the exact same methodology as above, if there are two Simons entitled to $25,000 per year (for 10 years) combined with only one Heather entitled to the same $25,000 (for 30 years), the transfer from any one Simon to Heather would be only $91,500 = ($212,750 + $212,750 + $487,250)/3 – $212,750, which is a smaller fraction of the value of their pension annuity at retirement and not as much to get enraged or excited about.

My point is that whenever you mix (i.e. pool) heterogenous people with different longevity prospects into one big pension scheme in which everyone gets a pension annuity for the rest of their natural lives, there will be clear winners and losers *ex ante*. And the sums being transferred from the latter to the former can be substantial. Ergo, the need for some sort of pension reform – namely the definition of age – on the grounds of fairness, especially if the lifetime gap between Simon and Heather continues to grow. And yet, to be clear, even in the current system Simon benefits from being part of the longevity pool. But my point is that it could be made even better if a biological age methodology were adopted for pension planning.

How Long Do We Live?

To get the reader thinking about how long Simon or Heather might actually live in retirement – versus the hypothetical 10 and 30 years I assumed earlier – consider the following data in Table 3.2. The world has approximately 451,000 people alive today above the age of 100 (a.k.a. centenarians). The country with the most centenarians is the U.S., with an estimated 72,000 of them. This might be surprising to readers who would expect Japan – with its staid image of old people – to have the most, and they do have the highest percentage per 10,000 citizens. But in terms of sheer numbers, Americans win this particular award. As you might expect,

41

the majority of the 72,000 (in the U.S.) are females (like Heather) versus males (like Simon). In fact, the ratio is about 4 to 1, that is four female centenarians for each male centenarian.

Table 3.2: Centenarians Around the World		
Location	Number	Per 10,000
China	48,000	0.3
Japan	61,000	4.8
USA	72,000	2.2
Canada	6,000	1.8
World	451,000	NA
Source: Pew Research Center (www.pewresearch.org)		

So, you see, there is a (small) chance that a generic male Simon might live longer than a generic female Heather, but the odds are small. And, if we happen to know that Simon's in poor health relative to Heather, the odds are even slimmer. At this point in the narrative you must still be thinking there is no way Simon wins.

Enter Longevity Risk

But what happens if we incorporate longevity risk or horizon uncertainty into our straw neighbors? Well, as I noted, there is a small probability that Simon lives for more than 10 years beyond age 75 and/or that Heather dies before age 95, and the exact terminal horizon is unknown in advance. In that case, the *ex post* transfer of wealth from Simon to Heather would be less than 60% of the value of his pension annuity. In fact, there is a (very) small probability that Simon actually outlives Heather and the *ex post* subsidy is in reverse and she paid for him. Again, we won't know until all the Heathers and Simons are dead.

But here is my next point. The pension annuity they are entitled to provides them with more than just a periodic cash flow or income, it provides them with longevity insurance, which is quite valuable and no less important than the life insurance I discussed in chapter #2. Moreover, the value or benefit of any type of insurance can't be quantified in terms of what might happen on average. It must account for the tails or edges of the distribution.

To the issue of fairness, consider the fact that we happily buy car insurance, home insurance and even life insurance in which the expected discounted value of the monetary benefits are less than what we pay. And yet, it makes perfect financial sense to do so. Why? It's about protection. Allow me to describe this in a way that a financial economist would prefer. Would you be willing to receive less than what you paid *on average*, but where the big payouts occurred in the states of nature in which you need and subjectively value them the most? Most economists would answer with a resounding yes. *On average* you don't die from the flu, you are never in a car accident and your house never floods. *On average* bad things never happen and insurance is wasted. But you don't buy these things for the average. You buy them for the tails.

Yes, this might sound a bit technical and we now enter the realm of insurance economics and the utility value of risk mitigation. Let's go back to Heather and Simon. As mentioned earlier, their income annuity entitles them to more than a term-certain annuity for 30 and 10 years, respectively. They have acquired longevity insurance that protects them in the event they live longer than average. Sure, Simon would rather be "pooled" with people like him who share the same longevity risk profile. But even Simon is willing to be pooled with people like Heather if the alternative is no pooling at all.

So, who values this insurance more? Heather or Simon? Or is the insurance benefit symmetric? Stated differently, could Simon be gaining more (in utility) from pooling with Heather, even if he is losing on an expected present-value basis? My definite answer is yes, Simon could be winning (economic utility) even if he appears to be losing (dollars and cents).

But why?

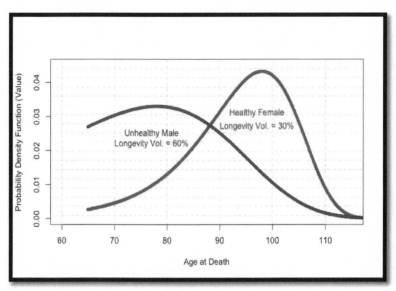

Figure 3.1

In a nutshell, his volatility of longevity is greater. Simon has a short life expectancy, but relatively speaking the range of how long he might actually live, expressed as a percentage, is actually larger than Heather's. Intuitively, the notion of Simon living 30 years instead of 10 years is equivalent to 200% "shock" to expectations. It's unlikely, but in the realm of possibility. In contrast, Heather who is expected to live 30 years will never experience a 200% shock. This would imply she lives 90 more years (from age 65) to the age of 155. It simply won't happen. The odds are zero. Ergo, Simon's volatility of longevity (in relative percentage terms) is higher than Heather's. That's biostatistics. But from an insurance economics point of view, it implies that Simon values the risk pooling benefits of the pension more than Heather does.

Figure 3.1 is an indicative picture of the volatility of longevity and, in particular, a comparison of a (sickly) Simon versus a (healthy) Heather's longevity prospects. For those readers interested in the (more detailed) mathematical argument underpinning this statement, I refer them to the references listed at the end of this chapter.

What is the bottom line for all of this? Well, the risk-adjusted transfer from Simon to Heather isn't as large as the expected dollars themselves indicate because Simon's volatility of longevity is larger than Heather's. Does it completely negate the fact that Simon will be receiving payments for 10 years (on average) and Heather will be earning them for 30 years (on average)? No. Not completely.

Of course, Simon is a euphemism for all the unhealthy males or individuals who retire and aren't expected to live very long, whereas Heather represents retirees with very long life expectancies. At this point I should like to make it clear that this isn't a matter of sex or gender, although it's an easy way to think about it. As I noted in the introductory chapter, there is a growing body of evidence that we can use to identify the Simons of the world *ex ante* (i.e. in advance, not after the died early in retirement) based on various biomarkers of aging, as well as the size of their wallets and magnitude of their income.

For example, a study published in the *Journal of the American Medical Association,* in 2016, documented a noticeable gap in life expectancy between U.S. taxpayers in the lowest income percentile versus the highest income percentile. At the chronological age of 40, taxpayers in the lowest income percentile have higher mortality rates and are expected to live 15 years less than taxpayers in the highest income percentile. More importantly, this is regardless of gender.

To quote from the article, "Men in the bottom 1% of the income distribution have an expected age at death of 73, whereas women in the top 1% of the income distribution have an expected age at death of 89." I'll return to this gap in life expectancy between rich (income) and poor (income) in chapter #5 when I dig into the mechanics of calculating biological age. Okay, the gap between the fortunate versus unfortunate groups is 16 years and not 20 years, but the gap could easily be larger if we rely on more than income alone. Add some additional biomarkers of aging and 20 years might be an underestimate.

One thing is very clear, and can be expressed using the language permeating this book. Individuals in the lowest income percentile have a biological age that is much greater than individuals in the highest income percentile, even if their chronological age is exactly the same. Pension schemes with very large pools of heterogenous (i.e. different type) people, transfer wealth from the unfortunate (who die early in retirement) to the fortunate (who live longer.)

And, even if we consider the fact that the less fortunate retirees are subjected to greater relative longevity risk – as illustrated in Figure 3.1 above – one still has to wonder if this is the proper way to design a pension scheme. Assuming you see the problem, this is one of the reasons I would suggest eligibility ages should be adjusted for biological age, even if you think it's fair that Simon pays for Heather. More to come in chapter #7.

Of course, there is a broader issue – that I haven't really discussed – which is how much of Simon's or Heather's retirement income should come from pensions that contain longevity insurance, that is, life annuities? That's coming up in chapter #4.

Sources and References

An expanded version of this chapter, with the economics and mathematics to prove it, is available and cited as (Milevsky, 2019). In that article I show that the volatility of longevity is higher for individuals with lower incomes – and higher mortality rates – and is linked to the fact that their mortality *growth* rate is lower. This might seem counter-intuitive at first, but you actually age faster than someone with the same chronological age as you, if have a higher mortality rate. Either way, you value pooling more.

The volatility of longevity is related to the compensation law of mortality (CLaM), introduced and explained in (Gavrilov & Gavrilova, 1991). The study linking income to mortality rates is cited as (Chetty, et al., 2016).

Finally, one of the earliest (and widely cited) economics articles examining the possible transfers of wealth from shorter-lived (poor) to longer-lived (rich), within the context of government pension plans, is (Brown, 2003). He was the first to make the point, which was then echoed in (Diamond, 2004), that the utility gains from pooling longevity risk were (still) positive in the late 1990s, despite the loss in expected wealth. My above-mentioned article (Milevsky, 2019) confirms this is the case, based on the recent data presented in (Chetty, et al., 2016).

4. Insurance Allocation

Why 9% of your income should be (expected to be)
wasted and how insurance is like phosphorus.

I started with life insurance (chapter #2) and moved on to pensions and the longevity insurance it provides (in chapter #3). In this chapter I would like to discuss insurance more generally, and how it fits into your financial lifecycle.

Regardless of whether it's for our life, car, health, house, vacation, engagement ring or anything else we value, the concept of insurance is a wonderful invention, one we are inclined to both love and hate simultaneously. A select few of us get to see its support in action – when we make a claim – but we all (mostly hate and) pay its cost. In a sense that's the challenge of promoting insurance. We benefit collectively, while the average person doesn't get a reward or return from the premiums they paid.

According to the U.S. Federal Reserve Bank, the median household income in the U.S. was close to $60,000 per year in 2018. Of this amount, I estimate that approximately 9% was spent on pure insurance, which is a global average. So, if your family earns the U.S. median income, then you are spending $5,400 every year on products you mostly don't want to purchase but that you need anyway. It sounds paradoxical and requires explanation, but first let's look at where this money goes.

As you can see from Table 4.1, the major spending categories tracked include auto insurance, property insurance, travel insurance, extended warranties, premiums on term life insurance policies, other properties and casualty. That's pure insurance. The table does **not** include products with a savings component, such as whole life, universal life or health (insurance) accounts. The unifying link for all items in the table is that if you don't use it by the end of the period, you lose it.

Table 4.1: Typical Insurance Products & Spending		
Product Type	Annual	% of $60K
Auto Insurance	$1,500	2.50%
Home Insurance	$1,080	1.80%
Term Life Insurance	$850	1.42%
Extended Warranties	$560	0.93%
Other Property & Casualty	$1,400	2.35%
Total	$5,400	9.0%
Source: Author (rough) calculations		

Now, I'm not here to debate whether the 9% of household income is too much to spend on insurance. In fact, for wealthier households, it might not be enough. Also, many consumers buy the wrong type, and others don't have a choice, since the bank or government mandates coverage. So, the 9% spent is quite loose and more of a global average.

Nevertheless, you really don't want to use or make a claim on any of these policies. Honestly, do you want to be in a car accident? Itching for your basement to flood? Looking forward to the vacation being canceled due to illness? I presume the answer to all of these calamities is a definite no. And yet, if disaster strikes, the policy is there to protect you. That's the love/hate nature of insurance. You hope not to use it.

In other words, it's quite logical to spend money on something you never want to use before the fact. But, if bad things happen to your precious assets, the **9%** will look like a bargain. It's not an investment *per se*, so the internal rate of return (IRR) isn't the metric that should be used to assess the value of protection. Insurance isn't an investment and one shouldn't use investment metrics to gauge its value.

Not on the Radar Screen

Interestingly, if Table 4.1 lists the major insurance categories, then there is something missing from the table displaying what Americans are spending on their insurance premiums. Do you see anything obvious? Well, as you age, one of the largest and most expensive items on your family balance sheet is your nest egg, that is, your retirement fund. If you don't have a guaranteed defined benefit (DB) pension, like the one I described in chapter #3, then chances are that you have a nest egg or retirement fund that you plan to convert into a personal pension. It too should be insured.

It might be worth hundreds of thousands and possibly millions of dollars, which is much more than the value of your car, basement or vacation. I can't seem to find any organization or agency that reports information on how much is spent on this sort of insurance, the same way auto or home insurance is presented. Yes, there is data on how much money is invested in fixed and variable annuities which contain an element of insurance, but nothing that breaks out exactly how much is spent to protect the nest egg. Sadly, it's just not on the radar screen of items that need protection. But it should be.

Now, in the olden days before formal insurance companies and policies, people were fully exposed to natural hazards (e.g. fires, floods and storms) as well as human-made hazards (e.g. theft, wars and even stock market crashes). In those times all people could do was pray, which might explain its popularity before insurance companies became prevalent in the late 17th century.

In fact, there is an amusing story about the famous English diarist Samuel Pepys that took place in the year 1666. It appears in his diary under the date of September 4, 1666. On that day, upon hearing that the great fire was spreading in London, he and his nextdoor neighbor Sir William Penn (founding father of Pennsylvania) rushed to bury their precious wine bottles and best cheese in their backyard – yes, cheese – and then proceeded to pray.

That was the era before insurance schemes and reliable policies. Incidentally, just a few years later, in the mid-1690s, the insurance market developed in London (think Lloyds, for example) and today there are better ways to protect your cheese, wine and eggs…as well as your nest egg. From this vantage point, old practices seem primitive. In the not-too-distant future we might look back and wonder why so many people didn't bother to protect their most valuable asset.

So, yes, insurance is expensive, but my main point in this particular chapter is that perhaps it's time to **reallocate some of the 9%** in your annual insurance budget to cover the risks that really matter as you get older. You are going to be spending 9% of your annual income on products you hope never to use – again, insurance – so you might as well spend and allocate this money more intelligently. Let some older policies lapse, drop the coverage and use the money for something else. I did so myself and will explain how in the next section.

Deferred Income Annuity (DIA)

One can think of longevity insurance as a bet that you will live to some advanced age, but in contrast to betting on some sporting event like the super bowl (for example), the bet actually helps your financial situation regardless of whether you win or lose. That's insurance. In particular, what I am referring to is that I wagered $5,000 that I would live to be 80 when I was only 47. And, in contrast to all the other insurance policies I listed in Table 4.1, that $5,000 is an insurance premium I very much hope does not go to waste. I very much want to get to age 80. Okay, let me explain the mechanics.

At the time, I deposited (i.e. bet) $5,000 with an insurance agent who accepted the money on behalf of an insurance company (i.e. a casino, if you wish). The company has invested the money for many (many) years. The way the insurance works is as follows.

If I survive to age 80 the insurance company has promised to send me exactly and precisely $2,160 per year in monthly instalments of $180 dollar – and increasing by 1% per year – for the rest of my natural life. If you think about this deal, it's a type of private retirement pension plan like the one that I described in chapter #3. It just doesn't begin until age 80.

There is a downside, though. If I die before age 80 my wife and kids receive absolutely nothing. I didn't pay for extra survivorship benefits or money back guarantees. But, the 1% increase per year once I do get to age 80 provides a measure of inflation protection. If I make it to 81, I'll get $2,182 for that year and, at age 82, I'll get $2,203 per year, and so on. In fact, after 28 monthly cheques – that is, if I live to age 82 and a third – I will have received my entire $5,000 back. I win, in a simplistic (not adjusting for time value of money) sort of way. This, ladies and gentlemen, is exactly what I mean by the phrase *pure longevity insurance*. It's the real deal, and I bought some because I thought – at the time – that my biological age was much less than 47.

How Long Do I Have to Live?

The above math doesn't account for the interest I could have earned over the next 33 years, and age 82.33 isn't really the *economic* break-even point. A proper analysis goes as follows: Had I purchased a matching government bond with the $5,000, it would have grown by 2.5% per year to mature at $11,300 by my 80th birthday in 2047. Using this figure as the benchmark, the proper break-even point is between age 85 and 86, chronologically. After reaching that milestone, every check I receive from the insurance company is its money or, more accurately, other people's money.

Like any other income annuity, my fellow comrades in the longevity risk pool who don't make it to 85.5 will subsidize my income, as I sail into the later golden years. I really look forward to hitting age 80, contacting the company representative, informing them I'm alive and that I'm officially "putting in a claim." I look forward to doing that for many years. And, I know of no other insurance policy quite like that, one that I look forward to using. Needless to say, I would only do this with an insurance company that has been around for centuries and most likely to be alive when I reach 80.

Good Bet or Bad Bet?

Now, when I mentioned this peculiar wager to some academic colleagues of mine at the business school, the initial reaction was that I would have been better off picking the Detroit Lions to win the Super Bowl in that year. (Note: The Lions have never been to the big game in their entire franchise history.) Basically, to make a long story short, I was told by many that it was a dumb bet.

The investment gurus argued that I could earn more than 2.5% interest with a good portfolio of stocks and that my internal rate of return (IRR) was lousy. The demographers and statisticians told me that the probability of reaching age 85 (chronologically) was only 50/50, and I was taking a big chance and might get nothing. Most vociferously, the macro-economic experts with their crystal balls argued that interest rates were heading up "any day" now and this sort of longevity insurance policy would get cheaper if I just waited a little bit longer. (Actually, it gets more expensive as I get older.)

Isn't it odd how nobody says or argues these things when it comes to life, home, car and other forms of property insurance? In fact, I'm quite certain that the expected IRR on those isn't great either. Why does longevity insurance raise such ire? Well, I stand by my wager. In my mind, the $5,000 is neither an investment nor a reckless bet. It is a hedge, and I plan to do more hedging in the future. I have been adding money to this deferred income annuity or *longevity insurance* policy for the last few years.

You see, as I have alluded to in many places in the book, the $5,000 buys me peace of mind. It is protecting me against the financial cost of living a year or even a decade more than I expected and planned. Will I make it to the break-even age 85.5? Well, as I noted in the prologue to this book, my father didn't (missing it by three decades) but my grandfather did (beating it by over a decade).

I think I take care of myself better than either of them did – that is, I believe my biological age is lower than their biological age, when they were at the same chronological age as me. So, yes, I might be facing a 50/50 chance, but again, this should be viewed as financial protection that my biological age is much (much) lower and I will live much (much) longer.

Back to the investment gurus and their portfolio, whether or not talented money managers can beat 2.5% over the next 33 years misses the point. Yes, if I opted to invest $5,000 in a portfolio of stocks instead of the longevity insurance, I might end up with more money, or I might not. Moreover, the money I spend on home insurance or car insurance or on any other one listed in Table 4.1 – for which I have never made any claims – would have also done better in almost any mutual fund. That's not how to think about insurance, as I noted earlier in this chapter.

To the financial forecasters final point, although I'm willing to concede that short-term rates are likely to rise soon, who knows if and when long-term interest rates will increase enough to justify waiting. And, the long-term rate is the relevant number for pricing this sort of product. More importantly, I financed the purchase of this *deferred income annuity* by selling some of my long-term bonds earning a similar (paltry) yield of 2.5%.

Ergo, what I really did was financially engineer a swap in which I replaced one type of fixed-income security (coupon bearing bonds) with another fixed-income security one that also provided longevity insurance. After all, as you get older you too should own more (and safer) bonds. All I did was wrap some longevity insurance around them. Longevity insurance is really a wrapper of sorts, one that can be placed around any asset class, investment or even a service.

Long-Term Care 500 Years Ago

Earlier I mentioned Samuel Pepys and the lack of property and casualty insurance during the Great Fire of 1666. And, while it would be a few more decades until Pepys and his contemporaries could purchase such coverage, other forms of insurance were available well before the 17th century. For example, commercial travel insurance, especially for boats, has been sold for millennia. Another type of insurance that I haven't mentioned yet, is one which middle aged pre-retirees are gaining a renewed appreciation for in the 21st century. That is long term care (LTC) insurance. Interestingly, a variant of LTC has been around for hundreds of years and was quite popular during the early 16th century in England.

After all, wealthy people have always worried about where they would live and who would care for them in their old age when they became infirm. So, centuries ago retired people, or at least those few who could afford it, purchased something called *corrodies*. It was yet another type of longevity insurance, one that paid-out in services, not cash. As you can imagine it was quite useful back then, if you didn't happen to have a family or a social network to assist you with activities of daily living.

Now, at this point you might pause and wonder to yourself: Retirement in the 17th and 16th century? Who made it to those advanced ages hundreds of years ago? Didn't everyone die by 30? But the fact is that quite a few people actually did survive to their 60s and 70s, even after a lifetime of working. And, if they did, they could expect another decade or two in retirement. Indeed, the conditional life expectancy at retirement hasn't changed (i.e. improved) nearly as much as the life expectancy at birth.

Thomas Hobbes, who I'll return to in the last chapter of this book, described life as "solitary, poor, nasty, brutish and short" in the 17th century. This has given many people the idea that nobody ever made it to retirement. Well, that isn't quite the case.

Take a look at Table 4.2, which is based on the most recent mortality rates, side by side with the oldest mortality rates available in the U.S. Notice that life expectancy at birth in the year 1789 was less than 30 years, a la Hobbes, but by the year 2014 it had increased to 78.7 years, based on (unisex rate) mortality data from the Social Security Administration.

The point I am trying to make is that despite the horrifyingly high infant and child mortality rates, which resulted in the abnormally low life expectancy at birth, if-and-when people survived to the age of 70, they could expect another 10 years of life in retirement. In fact, those people could expect to die at the age of 80.

Table 4.2 Expected Remaining Lifetime in the U.S.			
At Age	**In 1789**	**In 2014**	**Gain in years (%)**
0 (Birth)	28.2	78.7	50.5 (179%)
10	39.2	69.3	30.1 (77%)
20	34.2	59.5	2.53 (74%)
30	30.2	50.0	19.8 (65%)
40	26.0	40.5	14.5 (56%)
50	21.2	31.4	16.0 (76%)
60	15.4	23.1	7.7 (50%)
70	10.1	15.4	5.3 (53%)
80	5.9	9.0	3.1 (53%)
90	3.7	4.5	0.8 (21%)
Source: Social Security Admin. and Murphy (2010)			

You don't believe the numbers? Well, think of the U.S. founding fathers and first few presidents, for example. Although George Washington died at the age of 67, the second president John Adams lived to 90, Thomas Jefferson (#3) lived to 83, James Madison (#4) lived to 85, James Monroe (#5) lived to 73, John Quincy Adams (#6) lived to 80 and Andrew Jackson (#7) lived to 78. As a matter of fact, the average age at death of the first seven U.S. presidents was 80. Oh, and the great Benjamin Franklin made it to 84.

Back to my original question. What did older people who reach these advanced ages centuries ago, do to finance their retirement years? Well, back to corrodies.

Let me take you back 500 years to England in the early 16th century. At the time, local churches, abbeys and priories got into an interesting side business – which today we might call the nursing home business. In exchange for an up-front lump sum, wealthy couples could secure a clean and safe place to live, subsistence and meals for the rest of their lives.

Records preserved at the National Archives in London indicate the contractual level of precision that went into making these arrangements. For example, one record (TNA E315/94) presents the contract signed by Mr. Ralph Bagshawe and his wife Agnes, both from Devon and presumably retired. According to the document, they paid Forde Abbey a lump-sum total of 20 pounds in the year 1533. Think of it as an insurance premium. In exchange, they were promised the following benefits per week: (i) eight wagonloads of firewood, (ii) four loafs of conventional bread, (iii) three units of coarse bread, (iv) five gallons of regular ale, and (v) two gallons of small ale. In addition, Ralph and Agnes were to receive two measures of fish and meat, per week, and a cash allowance of approximately 5.5 pounds per year, for life. Nice retirement for 1533.

When you look at all of this together, and considering they only paid 20 pounds for the entire list of benefits, I think they got a good deal – at least *ex ante* – on their peculiar type of longevity insurance, which is more like a long-term care policy.

Not unlike the mispriced long-term care insurance of the 21st century, many of these corrodies appeared to be a very good deal (for the buyer) at the time. According to economic historians who have created time series of basic goods and services in the middle ages, the cost of just a few years of bread, ale and some decent fish would have well exceeded the 20 pounds. On the sell side, the prelate managing the money – that is, the manager of Forde Abbey – didn't need an actuary to tell him that this sort of policy was unsustainable. The buyer of the corrody was getting a good deal at the time. But, like all deals that sound too good to be true, there is a limit to how long this mispricing can last.

Alas, the Good Times Didn't Last

Those who know their English history will recall that around the same time, in the early 1530s, King Henry VIII fell in love with Anne Boleyn. And, when the pope in Rome didn't allow him to divorce his first wife Catherine of Aragon, he took control of the Church of England and then *dissolved the monasteries.* Yes, the place where Ralph and Agnes were spending their retirement, together with other wealthy seniors who could afford it.

The king seized the building and grounds, expelled the prelates, priests and cardinals, and then sold the land to private citizens. Think of it as a type of financial default. Anyone entitled to the corrody was, effectively, kicked out. In modern-day terms, the nursing home was repossessed by the government and the inhabitants were turned out.

Now, even in the 1530s, wealthy people had lawyers and annuitants sued the government (or king) in the so-called Court of Accommodations, which was managed by Thomas Cromwell and his buddies. Those detailed and documented proceedings are the source of information about Ralph and Agnes, mentioned above.

Some claimants were able to secure compensation from the defaulted corrodies, while others were left high and dry. It's an interesting story of longevity insurance gone awry and takes us somewhat adrift of our forward-looking biological age. Back to present day, the modern lesson is that retirement is more than money and long-term care insurance is a risky business, as GE and other insurance companies have recently discovered.

Like Vitamins and Minerals

The U.S. National Academy of Sciences in Washington publishes recommended dietary allowances and reference intakes on its website. In addition to the usual *vitamins* A, B, C, D, E, K, they also recommend a number of *elements* for daily intake. For example, a typical 50-year-old male should consume 1,000 milligrams of calcium (for females it is 1,200) per day, 700 milligrams of phosphorus (yes, also used for incendiary bombs) and 11 milligrams of zinc (for females, 8 is enough.) There are other interesting elements on the list, such as copper, iron, magnesium and manganese. For the record, there is no mention of ale or coarse bread.

Now think about the following "allocation" question. Should you include phosphorus or zinc supplements in your "portfolio" of daily pills? Answer: If your regular diet consists of plenty of peas (phosphorus) and shellfish (zinc), then you are probably consuming more than the recommended milligrams per day. There's no need for more. But if you don't (or can't) enjoy those foods – or other dishes heavy in phosphorus and zinc – you should consider supplements. But remember, 700 milligrams of phosphorus per day is a good idea, 7,000 is unhealthy and 70,000 will incinerate your internal organs and kill you.

My point? The role of annuities and longevity insurance in the optimal retirement portfolio is similar to the role of these minerals and elements. Remember, I didn't invest $100,000 into the deferred income annuity. It was much less. A well-balanced daily diet includes a mix of copper, iron, phosphorus and zinc. All diversified retirement portfolios should consist of some cash, stocks, bonds, real estate, health insurance, long-term care insurance and some – but not too much – annuities (i.e. zinc or phosphorus). I like to think of it as a retirement cocktail.

So, if you are already entitled to a substantial annuity income, you don't need any more. If you will receive substantial Social Security payments relative to you and your family's income needs, or a corporate defined benefit (DB) pension, then you might be over-annuitized or over-insured. That group of people (and they may be larger than you think) do not need any more. Too many annuities – that is, income that dies with you – could kill you.

The Lifecycle Model

On a broader level, the question or debate about how much of your nest egg (or insurance budget) to allocate to longevity insurance is intricately tied to the issue of *when*. As I pointed out in chapter #2, when I discussed the Spanish influenza pandemic, a young (28-year-old) breadwinner with dependents should have had (more) life insurance compared to a 70-year-old who was retired.

Using the language of mathematics, the optimal allocation to life insurance – at least for risk management purposes – declines with age. Early on your allocation is quite large, perhaps with millions of dollars in protection, but as you age (chronologically as well as biologically), it should decline. Well, the same exact idea applies to longevity insurance in the form of annuities, but in the exact opposite direction. Figure 4.1 provides an illustration.

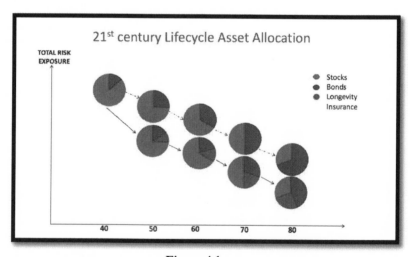

Figure 4.1

As you age, having guaranteed income for the rest of your life becomes more important and the benefits from pooling risk, that is the mortality credits I described in chapter #3, become greater. This, then, implies that you should allocate more of your nest egg or retirement account to insurance that protects against the cost of longevity. The red portion of the pie chart in Figure 4.1 increases as you grow older. For the record, the upper curve – without any red or longevity insurance – is the old (20th century) view of lifecycle asset allocation. Whereas the lower curve represents the 21st century view and perspective. In sum, like I did, think of buying some slowly over the lifecycle, as part of the process of saving for retirement.

Sources and References

The website of the Federal Reserve Bank of St. Louis, and specifically its data section, lists median income in the U.S. The numbers I quote are for August 2018. The Organisation for Economic Co-operation and Development (OECD) provided the number for total insurance spending as a percent of GDP, and a detailed report is available on its website as well. I assumed the same fraction was applied to household income. The source for home insurance and typical budgets was the Value Penguin website, and for auto insurance premiums the source was the Business Insider website, for March 2018. For overall life insurance premiums and sales, see the American Council of Life Insurers (ACLI) factbook. For the story of long-term care, King Henry VIII and the corrody purchase by Ralph and Agnes, see the article by Allison Fizzard, cited as (Fizzard, 2005). See also the book cited as (Murphy, 2010) for the source of the mortality rates in 1789, as well as for more information about the history of life insurance in the U.S., much before the Spanish Flu. See (Lewin, 2003), and in particular his chapter #7, for more on corrodies and other retirement provisions.

I reported and wrote about my purchase of a deferred income annuity in a *Wall Street Journal* article that was published online on January 29, 2015, under the title "Money on Seahawks or Patriots? No, I Just Bet I'll Live to 80." My first published research article on deferred income annuities (DIA), which I call advanced life delayed annuities (ALDA), is cited as (Milevsky, 2005). Many researchers and authors have subsequently written about DIAs (or ALDAs).

The most recent discussion or report on the topic is an EBRI Issue Brief, cited as (VanDerhi, 2019). VanDerhi examines the impact of allocating approximately 30% of your pension account balance to a deferred annuity (i.e. longevity insurance) that begins paying at the age of 85, which is five years after mine will begin.

One of the (many) impediments to voluntarily purchasing longevity insurance is that the benefit is only received many years after the premium has been paid. See the article cited as (Casaburi & Willis, 2018) which examines this issue in a completely different context (and I mean completely), where they report on randomized control trial (RCT) experiments with crop insurance in Kenya.

Casaburi and Willis demonstrate that the take-up rate for insurance increases – that is more people acquire the insurance – when payment isn't made up front but instead takes place at the point of harvest. And, despite the completely different context (and continent), one might argue that longevity insurance would be more popular if retirees paid premiums for the insurance (i.e. the annuity) much later on in retirement, perhaps even at the point of death. How would this work, you wonder? Well, there should be some way to engineer this with life insurance. Just a thought…

5. ACTUARIAL STATISTICS

In which I back up the provocative argument that your true age is really a very mysterious random variable.

Now that I have explained (in chapter #4) the core idea of "allocating" wealth to insurance and in particular longevity insurance, it's time to return to the second part of the title of this book, biological age. This chapter gets at the (numerical) heart and soul of the matter, where I explain how exactly medical researchers and other scientists compute biological age – the different methodologies involved – and how it differs from your chronological age. I'll try not to get too technical, but I do think it's important to discuss the measurement process as well as its many limitations and assumptions. Let me be crystal clear, writing from the perspective of the year 2020, it's a lot easier and less contentious to measure your chronological age. Indeed, there are no controversies about the process of subtracting today's date from your birth date. Not so with biological age. Warnings aside, here we go.

Generally speaking there are two (very) different statistical philosophies on how to compute a person's biological age. The difference between the two methodologies or viewpoints isn't just a matter of computational technique but is in fact motivated by one's background, discipline and field – as well as the intended usage of the number. And, although the statisticians themselves don't exactly use these terms, I'll label the two approaches the "living" methodology versus the "dying" methodology.

Stated quite simply – and perhaps too simply – in the former approach the benchmark for measuring true biological age is other people who are *alive*, and for the latter approach the benchmark is people who are *dead*. I'll explain both methodologies with detailed examples in just a moment, but for the record I am agnostic about which approach to use. They are basically two different ways of approaching the problem of measuring age, although I'll admit that my own research work with colleagues – referenced at the end of this chapter – has focused on the "dying" methodology.

I should also note rather uncomfortably that these two approaches might result in conflicting biological ages, given their distinctive focus. And, even within the two distinct statistical philosophies, there are methodological differences. So, in fact, there is a whole range of possible numbers for your biological age, depending on the approach. But this works in my favor, because my main point is that *you don't know exactly how old you really are.*

The Living Approach

Let's start with those who are living. Under this methodology a researcher would gather a very large group of people at a wide range of ages and collect samples of their saliva, blood and urine, and use those samples to extract various physiological and molecular (DNA, RNA, etc.) variables. These variables, which potentially could number in the hundreds, might include (5) red blood cell count, (6) hemoglobin concentration, (7) total cholesterol, all the way to items such as (72) fasting blood sugar levels, (73) urine specific gravity, (74) triglycerides, or – and this is an important one – (94) the average length of your telomeres, which I noted in chapter #1.

To be clear, the order and numbers I have placed in the round brackets are completely arbitrary and simply meant to remind the reader that there are many numbered variables, each represented by their own values. For example, your (74) triglycerides "number" measurement is likely between 50 and 200 milligrams per decaliter.

These *physiological and molecular* variables might then be augmented by *physical* variables (i.e. more easily measured, not requiring a laboratory) measuring things like (123) hand grip strength, (124) visual perception, or even (125) the number of missing teeth. There is a vector of numbers describing you, and it's getting longer every day.

Some enterprising researchers augment their dataset – for each one of the live people in the sample – with *social* variables, such as (179) number of friends on Facebook, or a binary variable measuring whether they like to garden (185). The theory here is that anything remotely associated with age – do you like the Rolling Stones? – can be added as a data point.

I confess that I have made up some of these elements in the above paragraph – I haven't see any studies on the Rolling Stones and longevity – but the limit of elements to include is really up to the researcher's imagination. But let's suppose they stopped at number 200, the last element being the number of Instagram followers a person has.

Once the data has been collected, each one of the elements is coded as a numerical score and every person in the sample is now associated with a vector of 200 numbers, including their gender. But the most important number, which one can visually imagine as being stored at the very beginning of this long vector, is the individual's *chronological age*. Again, I am describing the "living" approach.

To properly keep track of everyone in the dataset and the value of their elements, I'll denote the *i'th* person's (in the dataset's) *chronological age* by the symbol $y(i)$, and their long vector of physiological, molecular, physical and social characteristics by $x(j,i)$, where the index letter j ranges from 1 to 200 in this toy example. It can be as small as 1 element – telomeres or DNA methylation levels – if you want to only focus on those.

For example, to clarify the notation, the variable $x(179,98706)=100$ is saying that for individual number $i=98706$, the sample's *179*'th element (i.e. number of Facebook friends) was equal to a value of *100*. Likewise, the variable *x(7,55000)=205* would be interpreted to mean that the total cholesterol of the fifty-fifth thousand person in the sample was 205 milligrams per deciliter, etc. To repeat, the first number in the round brackets is the factor or element we are measuring; the second number represents the person. You might think of the second number in the round brackets as their unique Social Security or Social Insurance Number, except that confidentiality considerations would obviously preclude researchers from using those.

Okay. That's data entry and we now move on to the statistical part. The researcher then "runs" – that's the lingo used by statisticians – a multivariate (linear) regression of *y(i)*, as the dependent variable, on *x(j,i)*, the independent variables to obtain the best fitting function (actually a line), in the sense of "least squares." Variables that are not statistically significant are discarded (e.g. perhaps Facebook friends) and the multivariate regression is estimated again (and again) until the process converges on a collection of variables that really do relate (i.e. predict) the dependent variable, age.

And finally, *voila*, the best fitting equation becomes the formula for biological age. The individual errors in the regression are the gaps between a person's chronological age and biological age.

So, for example, if your estimated "best fitting" age – via the multivariate regression equation – was 35, while your chronological age was 50, the researcher would declare that you are really 15 years younger than your chronological age *because* the totality of elements in your personal vector appear closer to those of a 35-year-old than a 50-year-old. (So, all those followers on your Instagram account help make you appear younger. The equation maps the number of friend or followers into your true age.)

The so-called error in the regression equation (which isn't really an error in the baseball game sort of sense) is the difference between the chronological 50 and the estimated age 35. The error is *minus* 15 years. So, when you run your own parameters through such a multivariate regression – to measure your biological age – you want negative errors! (The error is the negative of what a statistician would call a residual.)

The statistically significant coefficients in this regression – remember that the researcher might have started with 200 but ended with only 30 – would then be declared as relevant biomarkers of aging. The sign of the coefficients, or you can think of them as factors, whether positive or negative, would determine whether scoring higher in those elements effectively makes you younger or older. Once again, biological age under the "living" approach is about finding groups of people you are most similar to.

For example, within the realm of physiological variables, consider uric acid, which was (imaginary) element number (97) in this multiple regression. A realistic range for this element is 2-6 milligrams (mg) per deciliter (dL), measured with a simple blood test. Now, its levels tend to be higher in people who are (chronologically) older – as well as in males versus females – so its coefficient in the multiple regression would likely be estimated to be positive. If your uric acid levels were higher than average, holding all the other hundreds of characteristics constant – including the gender element – then your biological age would be deemed to be higher than your chronological age.

Within the context of social variables, if the estimated coefficient on element (179), that is the number of Facebook friends, was negative and significant, this would imply that younger people (chronologically) tend to have more friends on average. Individuals in the dataset with less friends tend to be older (again chronologically). Ergo, if you have more friends than average, controlling for all other elements, your biological age is deemed to be lower. In the end, this statistical philosophy – which has been refined over many years – results in a formula (not necessarily linear), in which the relevant elements are loaded by the estimated coefficients and added together to derive your biological age.

A (More) Mathematical Way To Express Age

With a slight reformulation, I can rewrite the expression for biological age under the "living" approach, using the following multi-factor equation. It's not quite the regression representation I mentioned earlier – and the technicalities are beyond this book – but some readers might benefit from thinking about it the following way. This equation, which I promise is one of only two equations in this book, gets to the essence of the gap between your two ages.

$$BA = CA + \left(\sum_{j=1}^{k} \beta_j U_j \right)$$

The total sign (i.e. positive or negative) of the "stuff" in the round bracket will determine if your biological age is larger or smaller than your chronological age. And, if the total number in the brackets happens to be zero, then you are one of the very few on the diagonal line of Figure 1.1 in the first chapter; your BA is equal to your CA. But, I suspect most readers want the item in the round brackets to be as negative as possible – at least I do! – so that the resulting BA value is smaller than the CA constant.

Now take a closer look at the individual elements in the round brackets, that is, those factors that are being summed up and added. Each one of the (letter) *U* values represents a standardized biomarker of aging, and the Greek letter *beta* determines the relevant loading. For example, if the *18th U* value denotes your relative body mass index (BMI) measurement, it's *beta* value is positive. If your BMI is very large, multiplying by a positive constant and then added to your chronological age will result in an increase to your biological age, all else being equal, etc. So, I want zero, or even better yet, negative beta values on my personal U values that are larger than average.

Methodological Concerns

And here lies the problem or concern with the "living" approach. The implied biological age is based on how similar you are to other people, as opposed to directly estimating how long you are going to live or how soon you are likely to die. Yes, it's implicitly assumed that older people are more likely to die sooner, so the older your regression-measured biological age, the lower your life expectancy and the higher your death expectancy. But in the living approach mortality is not involved directly, nor does this approach care about what is likely to kill you. The basic dataset is a cross section of people at very different ages who are living at a given point in time.

Now, in some (recent) clinical studies, researchers have tracked large groups of people over time to examine if the older ones (biologically) are more likely to die or if they did not live as long as their identically (chronologically) aged neighbors, but it's an afterthought and obviously requires very long periods of time (decades, really) to establish. I'm not saying the "living" approach ignores death, but rather that it's based on people who are alive.

Here is the bottom line. The original formula for biological age is really about finding people you are most similar with and is primarily concerned with predicting functional impairments or the risk of chronic diseases. As one researcher put it to me, "We are interested in predicting and maximizing health span, not necessarily lifespan," which is why death and mortality rates aren't the focus of their attention.

There are other concerns with using the *"How similar are you to other people?"* approach to measure your true age, mostly related to the statistical significance of regressions when you have multiple independent variables, as well as concerns about linearity assumptions technical minutia I shall not get into.

For example, 20-year-olds are supposed to have many Facebook friends, but does it mean that if you have less, your biological age is older and you have a lower life expectancy than other 20-year-olds? It sounds ridiculous, which is why being similar to old people (in some ways) won't necessarily kill you.

Nevertheless, I have described an extremely fertile and popular area of research. Almost a month doesn't go by without some researcher uncovering another variable or element that predicts age. The original study of biological age – which go back decades – started with this "living" approach, and the tradition continues.

Most recently, *Science* magazine reported on researchers who found a link between the number of so-called *Eubacterium hallii* microbes in your intestines and your age. The data came from the American Gut Project (yes, this exists.) Using the language and notation I introduced earlier in the chapter, bacteria in your gut might be element number (201) in the regression, which apparently predicts age just as well, or even better than, the other 200. The hunt for biomarkers continues.

As noted, the search for true age has been ongoing for almost a century. One of the first elements to be identified as a proxy for age was farsightedness (a.k.a. presbyopia). The older you are, the harder it is to focus on objects that are close by. The prolific Polish mathematician Hugo Steinhaus – of the famed Banach-Steinhaus theorem, for all you math geeks – argued that farsightedness was a proxy for aging and life expectancy back in the year 1932. His early work on aging is still cited by biomarker hunters in the 21st century.

Decades after Hugo Steinhaus, the World Health Organization (WHO) hosted a conference in 1963 (in Kiev), dedicated to finding suitable methods for determining and defining biological age. This then spawned a literature of hundreds and possibly thousands of papers in the 1960s and 1970s. Many of them displayed the (famous) picture in which chronological age is the x-axis, biological age is the y-axis, and everyone in the dataset sits somewhere in the plane. For the most part, these papers have adopted the "living" approach.

It seems the race for biomarkers of aging – that is elements that have predictive powers, all else being equal – has intensified in recent years, especially considering the next natural step, which is to try to modify or reduce your age by assorted interventions.

In fact, a few years ago, the American Federation for Aging Research (AFAR) published a series of guidelines or criteria for biomarkers of aging. These criteria include some obvious ones, such as the test or measurement process shouldn't harm the subject and should be easily replicable. More importantly, AFAR stated: "It must predict a person's physiological, cognitive, and physical function in an age-related way. In other words, it must predict the future onset of age-related conditions and diseases and do so independently of chronological age."

Again, many of these researchers are focused on the general topic of healthy *aging* as opposed to measuring mortality rates or estimating the number of times you will circle the sun before you die. They want to predict much more than simply how long you will live. They are after quality of life, cost of care and preventative medicine. These are all noble pursuits, and quite important no doubt, but not quite what I mean when I talk about biological age in the context of pensions and annuities.

The Dying Approach

Now, in contrast to the living methodology, the "dying" approach is, as the name suggests, based on people who have died and is concerned with something that is much less complex than the multifaceted aspects of aging. Rather, it simply wants to predict time until death. No, these researchers don't collect blood and urine samples in cemeteries. Rather, the process begins by collecting data on *mortality rates* as a function of chronological age (obviously) and other characteristics or elements. For example, this might include the number of cigarettes the now-deceased smoked (from zero to a thousand) in the months and years before they died, or their body mass index (in kilograms per meter squared) before they died or their triglyceride level (in milligrams per deciliter) before they died.

Yes, these variables might sound and look very similar to the ones used in the "living" approach, but the difference is that to be part of this dataset you have to be dead, and the greater the number of dead (in the dataset) the better and more accurate the estimate.

I should note at this point in the narrative that the definition of a dead person – in the dataset or anywhere else – isn't as simple as one might expect. Usually one associates death with the absence of a heartbeat, that is, when the blood stops circulating. But there is another type (or definition) of death, namely brain death, which can be declared even if the heart is still beating. For example, if you are unconscious, incapable of breathing without mechanical assistance or have a brain wave scan that is flat, most doctors will declare you as dead, even if your heart is still beating. The definition of death is actually quite controversial and obviously related to the topic of biological age, but beyond the scope of this short book.

Needless to say, I won't attempt to measure or discuss the true age of a person whose brain stem is damaged beyond repair but who still has a pulse. Presumably, retirement income planning isn't the first thing on their mind in that state. Although, if you are entitled to longevity insurance (i.e. annuity income) for the rest of your life, the contractual definition of death might be an important issue to your family and loved ones as well as to the healthcare system.

Anyway, with the short detour to look at death variables behind us, I'll clarify that the "dying" approach for measuring biological age also involves a regression process, but the dependent variable, denoted by $q(i)$, is now a mortality rate, as opposed to a chronological age. The statistical regression process is about finding elements that are associated with higher death rates, together with a formula that maps those elements into a mortality rate. In contrast to the living approach, chronological age is not the dependent variable, nor is anyone trying to predict it directly.

For example, the best fitting regression formula for your mortality rate might be estimated to include a variable which is one minus the ratio of the average length of your telomeres in your body (in units of nucleotides) to the number 10,000 (for example). So, if the average length of your telomeres is 9,900 nucleotides, then your forecast mortality rate is (1-99/100)=1% in that year, all else being equal. In contrast, if the average length of the telomeres in your body is 8,000 nucleotides, the one-year mortality rate would be 20%.

Of course, this is a simple toy example, but the point is to focus directly on mortality rates in the estimation process. In the dying approach, one can also focus on an individual's wealth and income as well – and I'll get to that later – but it's more common to focus on (obvious) factors that affect mortality such as alcohol consumption, smoking, body mass index, physical activity, quality of sleep, blood pressure, resting heart rate and perhaps even how much time you spend walking in a given day. All of these factors are tested to examine whether they impact mortality rates.

For example, some researchers in the UK (cited in the references) conducted a large-scale survey of the population in England, Wales and Scotland over the period from 1982 to 2009. The researchers asked (and measured the extent to which) people if they smoked, drank, exercised and so on. They found, quite unsurprisingly, that people who smoked had higher mortality rates (i.e. more likely to die during the 25-year period) and that smoking was associated with a 70% increase in mortality rates. Likewise, a resting heart rate above 90 beats per minute was associated with a 60% increase in mortality rates. Lack of physical activity (which was less than 120 minutes of exercise per week) was associated with a 39% increase in mortality rates. Elevated (i.e. obese) body mass index values were associated with a 32% increase in mortality rates.

This is just one of many possible examples of studies that focus on the "dying" approach to biological age measurement. Statistically speaking, they segment people into groups based on observable characteristics – track them over time – and see how these features affect mortality rates. These sorts of studies require more time since you have to track people (and you want some of them to die), but they do provide a better sense of what is likely to kill you or keep you alive.

Mapping Death into Age

There is one final technical and rather important step in the "dying" approach – because the measured outputs are probabilities or likelihoods of being dead or alive – and that is to convert the estimated mortality rates into actual biological ages. Think about it this way, if you are 50 years old, are overweight and have high blood pressure, you might be told that your mortality rate is three times the normal amount for a 50-year-old male, based on the above methodology. But, *how do you convert this information into an age?* Well, the answer can get rather tricky, but it is essential to the narrative and agenda for this chapter. The final piece of the algorithm to compute biological age involves something called the Gompertz law of mortality.

Laws of Mortality

Mr. Benjamin Gompertz, the hero of this section and who had a natural law named after him, was born on March 5, 1779, and died on July 14, 1865, in London, at the age of 86. Among other distinguished accomplishments, he was the chief actuary at one of the largest insurance companies in England, the Alliance Assurance Company, where he served for almost three decades. He also was a full member of the London Stock Exchange (LSE). He was a successful businessman, and actively involved in the sciences.

Benjamin Gompertz spent much of his research life examining records of death, and specifically the exact ages at which people died. Until Gompertz, scientists and researchers would compile or collect these sorts of records, but had never much considered extracting any forward-looking patterns or formal laws of mortality. They knew how many people had died and could attempt to predict how many might die in the next few years, but the entire activity was rather *ad hoc* in the early 19th century, when Gompertz first got interested in the matter.

To make a long story short, Gompertz discovered that the probability or chances of dying for an average person in the population doubled every 10 years (approximately) from adulthood until old age. Today, this time period is referred to as the mortality rate doubling time (MRDT), and is closer to seven years for the global population.

So, for example, if the probability of dying at the age of 50 is 5 in a thousand, then the probability of dying during the age of 57 was 10 in a thousand, again, approximately. This is all quite general and there are many caveats, but Figure 5.1 is a graphical illustration, updated to modern mortality rates. If the mortality rate is doubling every 7 years, it's growing by approximately 10% per year.

Interestingly, there is vociferous debate about the doubling time and whether it gets larger – that is the mortality growth rate slows down – after the age of 95. This would imply that the pure Gompertz rule underestimates the chances you'll actually reach a higher age and would therefore be too pessimistic when applied to retirees who are in their late 90s. Mortality rates do tend to decelerate at older ages, that is, the doubling time is longer after that age, although the exact age at which this takes place is still being debated. Of course, these are all chronological ages I'm talking about here.

In fact, when actual mortality tables are compiled for the very few supercentenarians, that is people who died at age 110 and beyond, it appears that mortality rates stop increasing altogether. Of course Gompertz didn't have access to high-quality data for centenarians, although he did allude to a slowing down of mortality. The debate on what happens to mortality at very advanced ages continues, although it's not directly relevant to measuring biological age at 65.

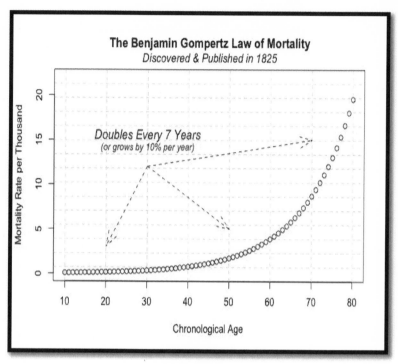

Figure 5.1

Back to our main agenda. The point of introducing you to this natural law, and its role in estimating biological age, is as follows. The Gompertz law of mortality – or formula – maps a chronological age into a mortality rate. It starts with a chronological age, and based on (i) the *initial* mortality rate and (ii) the mortality *growth* rate, or the inverse of the doubling time, it then outputs estimates of the mortality rate for that chronological age. To obtain the biological age I invert the formula and take as input the mortality rate and then solve for the implied age, which I will call the biological age.

Example: From Death to Age

Allow me to go back to two characters I introduced in chapter #3. Simon is 65 years old and has just been informed by medical experts that based on observable factors – such as the ones I discussed above – they estimate (i) a one-year mortality rate of 1.9/100, and (ii) a survival probability to age 90 of 22%. In contrast, Heather who is also 65 years old, is told by the same experts using the same forecasting models that the one-year mortality rate is 0.6/100 and the survival probability to age 90 is estimated to be 48%. Once again, Heather is in much better health than Simon. For the sake of benchmarking, both are told that the population *average* one-year mortality rates for an *average* 65-year-old is 1/100.

We can safely conclude that Heather is healthier than average and Simon is less healthy (or more sickly) than average, notwithstanding the fact that health itself is rather vague. Note that at this point I haven't said much about Simon or Heather, and even their gender shouldn't be assumed for now. The only thing that matters is that, although they have the same exact chronological age, their longevity prospects are quite different.

But to get to the essence of the matter. Both Simon and Heather would like to convert these forecasts or personalized mortality rates into a biological age, a number that is more intuitive and can be compared with their chronological age of 65. I concede that from the perspective of the question "Will I live for 25 more years?" the biological age number is rather meaningless. All that really matters is the underlying mortality rate, but for behavioral and psychological reasons having a true age is important to them personally, as I argued in a number of places in the book

It's obvious that Simon's biological age should be higher than 65 and Heather's biological age should be lower than 65. The question is by how much? Now, an insurance actuary might be tempted to (arbitrarily) select some population mortality table and then search for the associated chronological age x at which the mortality rate is 0.6/100 (for Heather) or 1.9/100 (for Simon). The actuary would report those x values as the corresponding biological ages for Heather and Simon.

Alas, this simple procedure has numerous problems or methodological issues. First, it's unclear what mortality table to use for this age set-back exercise. Second and more importantly, any exogenous mortality table is unlikely to be consistent with the second piece of information mentioned above, namely their 25-year survival rates. Recall that Simon was given a 25-year survival probability of 22%, but Heather's was 48%. In fact, Simon's survival probability implies an 8% growth in future mortality hazard rates, whereas for Heather it's 10.5%. It seems they could both obey the Gompertz law, but with different mortality rate doubling times (MRDTs). Third and more subtly, the gap in relative mortality between Simon and Heather is unlikely to persist for the next 25 years. So, mapping mortality rates into ages by inverting the x in the mortality function makes implicit assumptions about the evolution of mortality.

Nevertheless and without getting ahead of myself, part of the "dying" approach methodology is a parsimonious and consistent rule for mapping a set of mortality rates or projections for individuals – at any fixed chronological age – into a consistent biological age using a Gompertz model of aging for heterogenous populations. The precise details are spelled out in a (much more) technical paper cited in the references.

Needless to say, the "dying" methodology which I have described – and the mapping procedure I adopt – shy away from the truly difficult job of actually deriving or computing the heterogenous mortality rates based on observable biological, chemical or physical factors.

Rather, the mapping process assumes that someone (somehow) has created a forecast vector of mortality rates for groups of people who share Simon's characteristics as well as for groups of people who share Heather's characteristics. These characteristics might be income, wealth, nationality, ethnicity or perhaps even the length of their telomeres.

Wrapping Up the Differences

So, while I have positioned the "living" approach and the "dying" approach as different methodologies, they really are motivated by different questions. The former (living) wants to predict when you (personally) should start worrying about Alzheimer's disease, for example, while the latter approach – stated crudely – doesn't really care about what will be your cause of death or how many years you might spend in a nursing home. All it wants is the best possible estimate of how long you will live, which in the context of longevity insurance is really all that matters.

Numerical Results

With the methodology as well as the main idea behind us, Table 5.1 provides a summary of the results or output of the procedure for computing biological ages, under the "dying" methodology. For the sake of space, I have selected a subset of the countries for which high-quality mortality tables are available from the Human Mortality Database. A larger and more extensive list of countries is displayed graphically in Figure 5.2a (males) and Figure 5.2b (females)

Table 5.1: How Old Is a (Chronological) 55-year-old?		
Country	Female	Male
Australia	54.0	52.1
Canada	55.1	52.0
Germany	53.2	52.9
Italy	51.7	49.2
Korea	52.3	53.3
Russia	61.7	66.7
Spain	52.3	53.1
Sweden	51.8	47.9
UK	55.1	53.1
Ukraine	59.1	64.2
USA	59.6	57.6
Source: Milevsky (2019)		

Here is how to read the results and interpret what the table is trying to tell us. Imagine that you are a 55-year-old (chronologically, of course) female and happen to live in Canada. Assuming you are in average health (for a Canadian female), then your mortality prospects are quite close to average values in the developed world. Therefore, your biological age is very close to your chronological age, namely 55.1 years old. Stated differently, you are a mere 0.1 years older (biologically) than your chronological age.

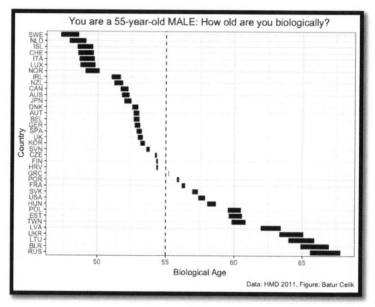

Figure 5.2a

But the situation is quite different if you happen to be an average Russian female who is 55 years of age, chronologically. Your longevity prospects are much worse than the global average, that is mortality rates are much higher compared to a Canadian female, for example. Using the C-age to B-age conversion algorithm, your biological age is 61.7, which is almost seven years higher than your chronological age. Stated differently, the average Russian female has circled the sun 55 years since she was born, but her body acts as if it has been 61.7 years.

But in contrast to the Russian or Canadian, the Italian female who is 55 years old chronologically is really 51.7 years old biologically. Her longevity prospects are better because her projected mortality rates are lower. Notice the gap between the highest number in the table (for females) which is 61.7, and the lowest number which is 51.7, or exactly 10 years. This is the gap in biological age around the developed world, for a female who is 55 years old chronologically.

So, what does it really mean to be 55 when it comes to pensions and retirement planning?

Alas, for males, the global gap is even more extreme, although the pattern is a bit different. We begin once again with a 55-year-old (chronologically) male who lives in Canada and is average in all observable dimensions. His longevity prospects relative to global rates are slightly better and his biological age is (only) 52 years. This might seem odd at first glance, as it appears that the Canadian male's biological age (52) is lower than the Canadian female's biological age (55.1). How can the male be younger than the female when they are both 55 years old chronologically? But remember, the mortality rates and values I am using to map or convert chronological ages into biological ages are segmented by gender. And, since the Canadian male is (much) healthier relative to the global male, his biological age is (much) lower. In contrast, the Canadian female isn't that much healthier, relative to the global female, so her biological age is nearly identical.

Needless to say, if we used one global (unisex, unigender) set of average mortality rates to convert chronological ages into biological ages, the Canadian male's biological age would always be higher than the Canadian female's biological age. It might be confusing and counter-intuitive, but as long as male and female ages are adjusted separately, the Canadian males will appear younger.

Moving down the table is the Russian 55-year-old male. His longevity prospects relative to (average) global mortality rates are quite bad, and his biological age 66.7 is almost 12 years more than his chronological age of 55. And, noticeably, his biological age is (still) higher than a Russian 55-year-old female. Stated more bluntly, his longevity prospects are absolutely atrocious on both a relative (around the world) and absolute basis.

In stark contrast to Russian males, the Swedish 55-year-old is 47.9 years old biologically, which is more than seven years below his chronological age. The intuition here once again comes down to mortality rates for males in Sweden, which are uniformly lower than global average rates and much lower than Russian mortality rates. Ergo, his biological age is reduced. Taken all together, notice how the gap between the highest biological age (66.7) and the lowest biological age (47.9) is almost 19 years. Figure 5.2a (males) and Figure 5.2b (females) shows the gap graphically, where the thickness of the horizontal bars is meant to visualize a range of values as opposed to the point estimate displayed in Table 5.1.

By this stage in the narrative I might be repeating myself, but will ask (once again) if chronological age should be used for pension and retirement planning?

Now, some astute readers might look at these numbers and think to themselves that all of this is just another way of saying that life expectancy for a 55-year-old Russian is much lower than life expectancy in Sweden or Canada, or almost anywhere else in the developed world. That is quite true and obviously the reason why the gap in biological age is so much larger in Russia.

For example, according to the OECD, the projected life expectancy of a 55-year-old Canadian female in 2014 was 33.0 years, whereas for a 55-year-old Korean female it was 41 years, which is a gap of seven years. So, Korean females have much better longevity prospects, and in our language would imply that the Korean female is (much) younger than the Canadian female, at the age of 55. But that is perfectly consistent with the story told in Table 5.1, although the exact numbers (or gap) depend on various methodological assumptions.

The OECD is projecting current mortality rates into the future and using those to compute life expectancy values, whereas what I have done is (i.) base the calculation on current mortality rates and averages, and (ii.) map them into a (universal) biological age.

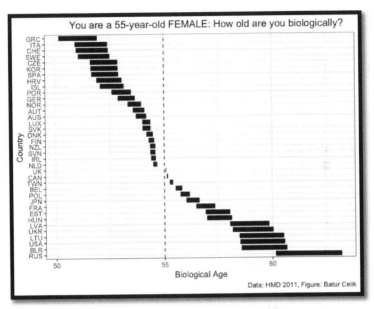

Figure 5.2b

It's Not Just About Countries

The bottom line is the same no matter how you look at it. South Koreans use the won and Canadians use the Canadian dollar. The exchange rate between the two currencies at the time of writing is approximately 850 won to 1 Canadian dollar. So, if you have units of currency in one country and would like to use them in another, you must convert by the appropriate exchange rate. All I'm saying is that the exact same process should apply to age as well. A 55-year-old in South Korea or Russia or Canada is not the same thing. Saying that you're a 55-year-old (male or female), without qualifying in what country, leaves the listener with a rather large and unknown gap regarding what your true (biological) age might be.

But this goes beyond citizenship or ethnicity or country of origin. Stating that you're a 55-year-old in any one given country still doesn't quite pin down your true biological age. As I noted earlier in this chapter, depending on the many physical, physiological and molecular variables, your forward-looking mortality rate might be higher or lower than your fellow countrymen and women. Whether you take the "living" approach or the "dying" approach to estimating biological age, the gap can be as large as 5, 10 or possibly even 15 years *within* countries as it is *across* countries. This phenomenon, which often comes with the label of mortality heterogeneity, can be quite controversial, as I noted earlier in the book, especially when the difference is correlated with income or wealth.

According to the same OECD report I noted earlier, even in long-living South Korea, the life expectancy of a male retiree at the highest income levels is five years higher than the life expectancy of someone at the lowest income level. In the U.S., this gap is much larger, according to the Chetty et al. (2016) study published in the *Journal of the American Medical Association.* It might be as high as 15 years for males, depending on how low (or high) one goes in the income distribution.

Figure 5.3 provides the results, using my measure of biological age. Notice that the "oldest" 50-year-old is in their mid-60s, and the youngest 50-year-old is in their late 30s. The only noticeable difference between these groups is their income, or the size of their wallet. Of course, the high-mortality group was also likely to include people who never went to college, never exercised and never stopped smoking. Those are correlated with higher biological ages too.

I'll end the chapter by repeating once again. How old are you, really?

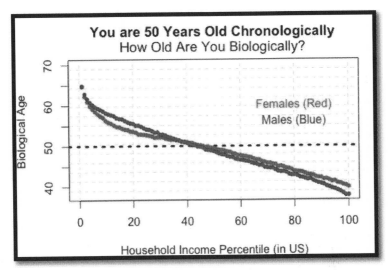

Figure 5.3

Sources and References

As with the prior chapter, the references contain a list of sources and articles that I found helpful when researching the concept of biological age. They may not be the definitive works in the field, nor highly cited, but I found them informative and interesting. In particular, see the articles listed as (Jackson, Weale, & Weale, 2003) and (Jylhava, Pederson, & Hagg, 2017), as well as earlier articles by (Ries & Pothig, 1984) and (Dubina, Mints, & Zhuk, 1984). The actuarial literature hasn't focused (as much) on the concept of biological age *per se*, although the insurance industry has obviously been adjusting ages, for pricing purposes, via the process of underwriting for a very long time. For actuaries this really isn't news nor is it debatable. For example, an article published over 15 years ago in the *North American Actuarial Journal*, written by an actuary working for a well-known re-insurance company (Held, 2002), begins with "Chronological age is clearly not the same as biological age."

As I noted within the chapter, what is problematic is how exactly to measure B-age, and whether it can ever be known with any degree of precision. More on this in chapter #7. If I can end with an analogy to physics, biological age is **not** the Higgs Boson from particle physics, which was *theorized* to exist in the 1960s (by Peter Higgs) but only *confirmed* to exist over four decades later. There really is no debate around the heterogeneity of health status at any given chronological age or the fact some people age faster than others. The controversial issue is (i) what information to use, and (ii) how to map or convert that information into a summary (true) age number. I suspect the debate will persist for quite some time.

The detailed algorithm for converting (period) mortality rates around the world, or for heterogenous groups within a country, is described in the article cited as (Milevsky, 2019), which also lists biological age values for other chronological ages and countries.

I mentioned the Organisation for Economic Co-operation and Development (OECD) and its estimates for life expectancy values across different countries and socioeconomic groups. These are based on two reports cited in the reference list as (OECD, 2014) and the more recent *OECD Pensions Outlook* cited as (OECD, 2018).

A recent article published in the *Risk Management and Insurance Review,* cited as (McCrea & Farrell, 2018), discusses how eight observable and common health variables I noted in this chapter (and mention in detail in chapter #7) can be used to adjust chronological age to arrive at a more accurate assessment of mortality rates for the purposes of insurance pricing. They claim that high-risk subjects (in their sample) have a biological age (using my terminology) that is 7.8 years higher than their chronological age.

6. ENGINEERING LONGEVITY

How old is your money? Is your retirement fund aging well? And why your portfolio's life expectancy matters.

So, the takeaway from the prior chapter is that your body has its own unique age, a number that doesn't care about what's written on your passport or driver's license. In 12 calendar months, you personally might be aging more or perhaps less than one chronological year and it can change over time. This chapter looks at the true age of something else, namely your retirement nest egg and investment portfolio. In fact, it too might be aging poorly and could die prematurely if it isn't cared for properly. Allow me to explain.

First, in the early chapters I alluded to the fact that the longest living people on earth reside in Japan – and their mortality rates are among the world's lowest – so they actually know a thing or two about planning for longevity. Although they are a nation that is 40% of the U.S. population (127 vs. 325 million), they have almost as many centenarians (67 vs. 78 thousand) as in the U.S. Even more impressively, 6 out of 10 supercentenarians (i.e. defined as those above the age of 110) on planet Earth live in Japan. With a low birth rate, the country is growing old very quickly, but it is still quite vibrant and healthy.

I focus on Japan and can actually attest to its population's longevity because I wrote this particular chapter while riding on a bullet train from Kyoto to Tokyo, which is a marvel of modern engineering, traveling at speeds of over 200 miles per hour. When I looked around the train, I felt quite young for a change. This was in contrast to my university job teaching undergraduates who make me feel very old. (The students seem to be getting younger every year.)

Back to your money, on a philosophical level a portfolio is a living and breathing organism with a finite lifetime in the decumulation phase of the lifecycle. And, while the equation for human longevity depends on many interconnected variables, as I explained in the prior chapter, portfolio longevity is primarily driven by only two factors: your investment returns and your spending rate. Withdraw too much or invest inappropriately and the portfolio will collapse faster than you can say Godzilla.

Longevity Equation for Money

There is a relatively simple equation that determines the longevity of a portfolio. It doesn't require anything as complicated as the advanced calculus needed to build a bullet train. Rather, it can be expressed mathematically in one line as:

$$L = \frac{1}{g} \ln \left[\frac{w/M}{w/M - g} \right]$$

In this equation, the letter L represents longevity in years, g denotes a real rate of return after taxes and inflation, w is a withdrawal amount in real dollars and M is the sum of money in your nest egg at retirement. Finally, the *ln* (thing) denotes the natural logarithm; which is simply a button on your phone and no cause for panic. So, in contrast to chapter #5's equation for biological age (which is associated with human longevity), here I present an equation for financial longevity (which can be associated with the biological age of your money.) Now, I concede that unless you are an amateur mathematician, this equation might not mean very much, so here is a simple example to see how it works.

Assume you are entitled to $40,000 in Social Security benefits – guaranteed for life and adjusted for inflation – in addition to a nest egg or portfolio of $600,000 invested in a diversified portfolio projected to earn 3% per year. Now, you would like to withdraw $50,000 every year to satisfy a total income need of $90,000.

The questions many people at this stage of life ask themselves are as follows. Is this retirement plan sustainable? *What is the longevity of the money?*

Well, if I plug or insert these numbers into the above equation, the withdrawal (w) is $50,000 and the initial portfolio value (M) is $600,000 so the ratio of the two (w/M) is a withdrawal rate of 8.33%, which is quite high, in my opinion, without doing any fancy math. But let's get an actual number. The next step is to assume a real after-inflation and fee rate of return (g) which I take to be 3% – for reasons I'll discuss later – and then compute the ratio inside the square brackets, which leads to 1.5625 units. The natural logarithm of this number is 0.46629, and dividing by 3% results in a left-hand side value of 14.9 years.

In other words, the portfolio will be exhausted within a decade and a half of retirement. And yet, as a healthy retiree you have a longevity of 25 years even if you aren't Japanese. Again, your money has a longevity of 15 years. This isn't a sustainable plan. You are relatively young, but your portfolio is getting old much too quickly. The money will die prematurely. It needs a longevity extension.

Table 6.1: How Long – in Years – Will Your Portfolio Live?				
W/draw	$400K	$500K	$600K	$700K
$40,000	11.9	15.7	19.9	24.8
$50,000	9.1	11.9	14.9	18.2
$60,000	7.4	9.6	11.9	14.4
$70,000	6.3	8.0	9.9	11.9
Source: Calculations at g = 3%				

So, here is the actionable item. If you can wait a few years until the nest egg (portfolio, financial capital, money) grows to $700,000 (for example) and then withdraw only $40,000 per year (for example), the same formula or procedure results in a portfolio longevity of 25 years. Now that number is in the same ballpark as human longevity. You have added a decade to the portfolio's life.

Now, to be clear, the portfolio longevity equation doesn't guarantee that your money will last for exactly L years, but it can provide a darn good estimate. It will be exactly correct in a universe in which real (after-inflation) returns are exactly 3% and withdrawals are constant year-over-year in inflation-adjusted terms.

If you don't like my numbers or assumptions, you can use your favorite economic and financial parameters. My point isn't to argue that 3% is a realistic inflation-adjusted return (it's actually a tad high, especially after investment fees). My point is that the math is transparent (replicable) and likely a sobering wake-up call to many retirees. It can also serve as a welcome license to spend a little more, if the longevity number (left-hand side of the equation) is very high.

Let me say this in a slightly different but perhaps more memorable manner. *You must ensure that the age of your portfolio – in the longevity sense – is lower than your biological age.* Your portfolio's life expectancy should be greater than your life expectancy. In my book, it's the secret to a sustainable retirement income plan. Retire when you are older, older than your money.

Deterministic Warning

Now, if you happen to have a Ph.D. in financial engineering (for example) and are wondering, *"Okay, he's playing loose. What about the second and third moment of the portfolio's longevity?"* Or if you read this and are itching to know about *"the entire probability density function of the variable L,"* then I suggest you take a trip to Monte Carlo, fire up the computer simulations and do some advanced calculus. But do this only after you understand the basic deterministic relationship.

In my mind the simulations and calculus are the version 2.0 of the lecture on retirement income planning. My motto is if you don't understand the underlying math, then don't use or quote it.

What does this have to do with longevity insurance? Well, consider the longevity of your money when the income or cash flow is actually coming from a pension or any other form of lifetime income annuity. For example, if you are drawing $40,000 under the terms of an immediate or deferred annuity, how long will the money last? Well, I would argue that for all intents and purposes its **longevity is infinite** because it will always last as long as your own human longevity. You don't have to use the equation at all for the money that is inside an annuity. *Its longevity is assured.*

In summary, you have a chronological age, a unique human longevity and therefore a biological age. Well, so does your financial portfolio. You can tilt the portfolio longevity equation in your favor by allocating some funds towards longevity insurance (i.e. a life annuity).

Insuring Two Longevities

As I alluded to above, the equation works nicely in a (fictitious) world in which investment returns are known and fixed. But that never happens, especially if you own a mixture of volatile stocks and bonds in your retirement portfolio – which you actually should if you want some growth over time.

So, in fact, the two greatest sources of economic risk that retirees face in retirement are related to (i) their true biological age, that is their human longevity, and (ii) their portfolio's investment return over their uncertain lifetime, which then ties into the portfolio's longevity.

Yes, of course, retirees face many other economic uncertainties, such as the increasing and unpredictable burden of healthcare, future inflation rates, income taxes and even children and grandchildren with unexpected financial needs. But, most of these other sources are either smaller in scale, more predictable in magnitude or can be traced back to the *big two retirement risks.*

Now, think about it carefully. If by chance your personal investments happen to (get lucky and) earn extraordinarily high returns, then you will likely have more than enough money to cover your other retirement obligations and costs. Likewise, if your personal longevity or lifespan is much shorter than average (i.e. your true biological age is much higher than your chronological age), then as ghastly as this might sound, the good news with hindsight is that you didn't really need that much money to finance your retirement.

Conceptually, this two-dimensional space or continuum can be envisioned in the following way. The human longevity and financial market vectors (lines) partition a square into four distinct quadrants. Look carefully at Figure 6.1, before you read on.

The east side represents above-average longevity and the west side represents the opposite. Living an exactly average lifespan, places you directly in the middle – but remember nobody is average. Focusing on the vertical portfolio performance, the north represents your investment portfolio achieving above-average return and the south is, as the word suggest, under-average investment performance.

Most financial plans are geared or calibrated to the intersection of these two lines, which represent an average life (e.g. 80 years) and average returns after fees and inflation (e.g. 3% real). Of course, realized numbers will be all over the chart, or the two-dimensional plane of the figure.

A financial mathematician would describe the two dimensions or factors as being *orthogonal* to each other, which is just another fancy word for statistically independent uncertainties. These are risks that should be protected. Basically, there are four things that can take place over the course of your retirement, each with approximately a one-quarter chance of happening – and, more relevantly, each with a very different economic outcome.

Four Economic Outcomes

Let's go through each one carefully, and then I'll get to what this has to do with longevity insurance and engineering. The northeast quadrant represents a long and prosperous retirement in which you live (much) longer than average and experience portfolio returns that are well above average. Clearly, the risk exposure or economic damage in this *state of nature* is minimal. There certainly is no need to insure or protect against this outcome. It's a blessing in two dimensions. A long retirement is expensive, but the strong returns of your portfolio should be able to sustain the spending.

In the second quadrant, to the northwest, the portfolio has performed well above the expected average, but longevity or lifespans were under average. Remember. This is after the fact (or *ex post*). Once your retirement is over – and you have moved on to a better place – you can then look back and try to estimate what quadrant you landed in. And, while we can't describe the northwest outcome as a blessing in any dimension, the fact is that it isn't (or wasn't, in hindsight) a costly outcome. It certainly doesn't require insurance protection. The money lasted. The limited years of needs were met. At the risk of repeating myself, and to be clear, this is a hypothetical exercise in which we look back at the end of life and wonder – *in what quadrant did I land?*

Moving to the southwest region of your possible retirement plane, you'll see that in that box the investment portfolio and markets haven't performed as well as expected. This will have led to some financial stress, but the reduced longevity (i.e. you died early, so to speak) implies that this outcome won't be as costly from an economic point of view. To be clear, the third quadrant contains some risk for the sustainability of retirement, but it's likely manageable.

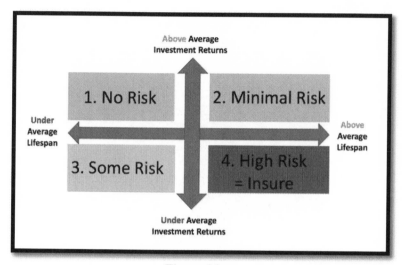

Figure 6.1

We now get to the main point of this entire exercise. You should now recognize that the most stressful retirement quadrant is in the southeast. This fourth quadrant represents the unpleasant outcome in which your lifespan was above average – with the associated higher costs of retirement – but market returns weren't enough to support the additional longer period of withdrawals. It is represented by the red box (for those of you seeing this in color) and in my opinion is an outcome asking for a longevity insurance solution. It's the *raison d'être* of many investment-based annuities with guaranteed living benefits sold by insurance companies and obviously quite popular with retiring baby boomers.

Protect Against the Worst Quadrant

So, here we are. This is precisely where market-contingent longevity insurance fits into the retirement income story. Up to this point in the narrative I have talked about one dimension, longevity. These products offer protection against two distinct events, each of which alone might not have as damaging an effect on retirement finances.

Now sure, in theory you could purchase insurance or protection against outcomes on the entire east coast of the plane, that is to insure against the cost of a long life regardless of how well your other investments perform. You could also purchase protection on your entire portfolio (e.g. using put options). But, these sorts of strategies would be overprotecting, in my opinion, and likely more expensive than necessary. Yes, they are simpler, more transparent and easier to explain – but might not be more efficient. Remember, if your portfolio performs above average, which is a northern outcome in the figures, you likely have more than enough to sustain your lifestyle. Be surgical with your longevity insurance.

In sum, I am often asked by financial advisors what problem a modern annuity product is actually solving or what "question" and need it is trying to answer and meet. In my opinion, and with the figure in mind, the value proposition of market-contingent longevity insurance resides in the unique combination of two-dimensional protection embedded in its DNA. Such a product will implicitly protect against two distinct risks, each of which on its own would likely be more expensive. Or think of it another way, it's the cheapest way to protect your retirement in the southeast.

Sources and References

The main equation in this chapter can be traced back to Leonardo Fibonacci, as discussed in (Milevsky, 2012). The idea of jointly insuring an investment portfolio as well as human longevity, displayed in Figure 6.1, really goes back to an Arrow-Debreu view of the word, which should be familiar to most graduate students of economics.

7. RETIREMENT POLICY

---

*How a note from your doctor could start your pension
and why a Japanese is younger than a Russian.*

In Moscow, Russia, during the summer of 2018 when most of the world was watching Cristiano Ronaldo's lackluster performance on the field, President Putin decided to push through a new decree that he hoped wouldn't get much notice during the soccer hoopla. No, he wasn't planning to annex a neighboring country or make another dissident disappear. He wanted to do something far more controversial, apparently. He planned to increase by a few years the official age at which Russians could draw their state pension. The public reaction was explosive.

At the time, strict Russian law – yes, a bit of an oxymoron – stated that men could begin drawing their government pension at the age of 60 and women could start their retirement income at the age of 55. Now, if you have been following some of the numbers I mentioned in prior chapters, and in particular the discussion in chapter #3 on pension economics, those chronological ages might appear somewhat low. Typical chronological ages for retirement pension entitlements are 65 to 67 in North America. So, at first glance, the proposal to (slowly, very slowly) increase eligibility ages in Russia by approximately five years, seems quite reasonable.

For comparison, according to the World Bank, between the years 1995 and 2018 a total of 57 countries around the world set in motion legislation to increase the retirement age. I'm talking about countries like Kazakhstan, Ukraine and Morocco.

But the Russian public disagreed and, in hindsight, President Putin was quite clever to (attempt to) introduce this proposal while the public was distracted by goals.

As part of the public safety measures for the world cup – and to assuage foreign tourists who might be concerned about soccer hooligans – public protests and marches were outlawed in Moscow and St. Petersburg during the period of June and July. So, unhappy 50-year-old Russians who were living in the major (soccer) cities were limited as to how they could express their frustration. The typical and long-standing tradition of taking their grievance to the street wasn't an option. But smaller cities – without any scheduled soccer games – were fair game and, from Tomsk to Komsomolsk, Russians gathered to shout their displeasure at President Putin's pension proposals. According to one survey conducted at the time, 89% of Russians opposed the pension reform, and President Putin's approval rating took a big hit as well.

And yet, despite the global trend towards higher and older retirement ages, I would argue that these protesters had a valid point. Recall from the extensive discussion in chapter #5 that mortality rates in Russia are much higher than most other (developed) countries in the world. Life expectancy in Russia is somewhere around 64 to 66 years, depending on the region, which is a decade or two less than North America and Europe. Or, using the language and ideas from this book, the biological age of a 65-year-old Russian might be as high as 85.

In other words, most Russians (and especially males) will not live long enough to enjoy the fruits of the retirement pension and at most might be able to cash a few monthly checks before their human longevity runs out. They are an extreme case of the sickly Simon I introduced in chapter #3. They paid for something they might never receive. Rightfully so, they expressed their frustration.

Now, it's one thing to propose higher retirement ages in Japan, where mortality rates are (much) lower and most men and (especially) women live into their late 90s. But in Russia, becoming a centenarian is unheard of and seeing the 90s is equally rare.

The Age Fix

If President Putin had asked me – full disclosure here, I am not a consultant to the Russian government or its financial authorities – I would have suggested that he design and explain his pension reforms using the framework of biological age. In fact, I would give the same advice to any head of state or government pension agency that might inquire. I would start the narrative with Table 5.1 in which you can see the different (and true) age of someone who is 55 years old. In particular, recall that in Russia, a 55-year-old male is biologically 66.7 years old. Not far from Russia geographically, in Sweden, the same 55-year-old would be 47.9 years old biologically. The absolute concept of chronological age is rather meaningless, as I have argued in many places, and at the very least it should be adjusted for "age inflation" or deflation, from a Russian perspective.

In the United Kingdom and the Netherlands, governments and policymakers have recognized the "age inflation" component of the problem and have implemented a system in which the national retirement age is linked or automatically pegged (using an inflation term) to population life expectancy. A typical pegging formula looks something like this: national retirement age RA is equal to life expectancy LE minus 20 years, or $RA = LE - 20$. So, if and when government actuaries or statisticians announce that average life expectancy has increased, from say 86 years at birth to 87 years, the national retirement age increases a year to 67. There is no need for special legislation, renewed lobbying or public debate. Like a thermostat in your house that adjusts the furnace and air conditioning based on the latest temperature reading, it's an automatic peg forever.

So, I ask, why not do the same sort of thing on an individual level and accounting for individual life expectancy? My formula would look even simpler: $RBA = 65$, namely retirement is at 65, *biologically*. As soon as you can prove (with a note from your doctor, perhaps) that you are 65, you can turn on the pension.

Is it Fair?

At this point some readers might accuse me of promoting state-sponsored theft, or under the sunniest of lights, advocating a policy that is patently unfair. After all, I am effectively proposing that a government compel someone who happens to have hit the genetic jackpot (or lucky sperm club) and is 50 years old chronologically, albeit with a biological age of 40, to work for 25 extra years. In contrast, someone who is the same 50 years of age, might only have to work for another five years and still be entitled to the same retirement pension income if their biological age happened to be much higher. Heather will have to work longer than Simon.

Is this ethical?

Well, I'm certainly not a moral theorist or professional ethicist, but I do happen to have one close by. My brother Jonathan has some expertise in these matters. So, I asked his thoughts on the dilemma. Would it be fair to design a pension system in this manner? Well, it seems that the answer is yes – at least to a philosopher.

In fact, he responded by invoking the notion of a "social contract", meaning the concept that by living in a given state one tacitly agrees to the state's laws and has a basic responsibility towards the government. He said that the idea is a very old one, going back to Ancient Greece. The philosopher Plato, in his work *Crito*, tells the story of Socrates, who is sentenced to death, and is presented with the opportunity to escape, but yet he feels an obligation to remain and accept the verdict out of a sense of obligation to his city and its laws. Even the term social contract is itself an invention of the Greeks. They used it to describe the law of the city and the obligation of citizens to follow that law.

More importantly and germane to the matter at hand, the responsibility that citizens have to their city differed from person to person. The duty to sit on a council, which is the ancient equivalent of today's jury duty, or to make a donation to charity, or to perform military service, depended on your personal circumstances, such as your wealth, social standing, and natural capacity. You can already see where I am (and he was) going here. Those who are more fortunate – in our case, that would mean having a lower biological age – would have a greater burden and responsibility.

One can take this argument one step further with the help of another social theorist, Thomas Hobbes, who was born in 1588, lived for a remarkable 91 chronological years in the 17th century and died in the year 1679. Hobbes was a contemporary of Samuel Pepys.

Having witnessed the instability of the Civil War, essentially a struggle between Charles I and Parliament, Hobbes recognized the need for a monarch's absolute power.

In chapter 20 of his book *Leviathan,* he writes that, in the frightful state of nature, human beings relinquish their right to violence against their neighbor, to their monarch, and in return they receive the monarch's protection. As a result of this right, which Hobbes viewed as divine, the monarch could exercise power over their subjects, in matters ranging from finances to military obligation.

Like the Greeks, Hobbes also believed that the responsibility of the monarch's subjects varied. This comes out in a point he makes about work and employment, a point that is very relevant to our discussion of state pension and retirement plans. Hobbes claimed that those who have "weak bodies" should be "provided for, as far as the necessities of nature require." But for those who have "strong bodies," he says, "they are to be forced to work."

So, taking Hobbes' ideas into consideration, I would refer to a socioeconomic contract as the justification for my biological age pension proposal. Our responsibility to society stems not only from relative peace we enjoy in the place where we have chosen to live, but also from the economic system of which we all decide to be a part of.

Then again, as Hobbes realized, our responsibility to the government is not something we share equally: one's personal responsibility depends on their natural capacities. And, since modern technology gives us a greater insight into our natural ability, it makes sense that the same data should be factored into the determination of what is expected of every citizen.

Bottom line, I don't think it's unfair to make some people work – and pay into the pension system – for longer than others. The above noted socioeconomic contract dictates that if you are the lucky individual whose biological age is lower than your chronological age, well, you ought to work for longer, compared to someone for whom this is reversed.

Could the System Be Gamed?

Arguably, yes, to a certain extent. If retirement pensions and income could be started as soon as your biological age hit 65, then some clever and nefarious tax payers might be inclined to cheat the system and actively increase their body's age, to get an early (and fraudulent) jump on their pension. Would anybody at any chronological age be entitled to start their retirement pension if their biological age hit age 65? Even if they had contributed very little to the pension plan? What if their biological age dropped back into the "working zone" after it hit the "retirement zone"? Would the pension be stopped. There are many unanswered questions on how this would be implemented and fraud would be at the very top of the list of concerns.

Perhaps readers envision a cottage industry of unethical testing facilities and doctors who – for a small fee – would provide you with an answer key to help pass the pension test and quickly hit 65. Might we see the emergence of "old" blood donors who you could hire to "bleed" for you?

A recent story along the fraudulent lines, one that garnered quite a bit of media attention, involves the famous Madame Jeanne

Calment, who died in France in 1997. Apparently, and this is the controversial part, she died at the astounding age of 122, chronologically. This number is the world record for the longest living individual (Bible matriarchs and patriarchs excluded) and currently viewed by most scientists as the upper limit of human longevity.

But questions have been raised about her true age, and some researchers are claiming her identity was stolen by her daughter during the war, in the 1940s, and that Jeanne really died decades earlier at the age of 97. I have no opinion – or longevity horse in the race – either way and don't want to delve into the controversy. But faking ages was quite common and acceptable during periods of war.

An entire generation of soldiers who fought in World War I were actually younger than their stated age. They lied upon enlisting, not to make themselves older for the sake of pension money but to be allowed to fight for their country. You see, there was a chronological age requirement of 18 to enlist. So, lying about your chronological age has an age-old history, which is why passports and birth certificates are designed with such extreme security in mind. Fake IDs might get you into a cheap bar, but don't try using them at the TSA checkpoint. Would a biochemical dating process be foolproof?

Well, let's think for a moment about what is involved in fooling the test and increasing your biological age. How would somebody convince a doctor (or a blood test) that they are much older than their chronological age? To answer that let's go back to some of the easy metrics that can be used to determine biological age. Table 7.1 lists eight obvious ones.

Would you be willing to change your lifestyle and adopt any of the eight suggestions in Table 7.1 on a sustained basis in order to start your pension? I'm not talking about an occasional cigarette, a few sleepless nights or eating a few more bacon cheeseburgers. It would have to be for a prolonged period of time so that it truly alters your body's chemistry.

Table 7.1: How to Increase Your Biological Age	
Suggestion	How to Implement
Drink Alcohol	More than 14 units per week
Smoke	Any amount of tobacco
Get Obese	Have BMI >= 30 KG/m^2
Be Sedentary	Exercise < 120 min. p/w
Sleep Badly	Less than 7 or >9 hours
Increase Blood Pressure	Hypertensive readings
Mistreat Heart	Resting heart rate > 90 BPM
Stay Put	Walk less than 20 minutes p/d
Source: McCrea and Farrell (2018)	

Table 7.1 doesn't include cutting down on fiber, fruits, vegetables and nuts. To make it work you would also have to increase your intake of refined flour, fried foods and omega-6 fatty acids. I hope you get my point. We aren't talking about faking a superficial injury for disability insurance. You really have to mess with your metabolism to increase that biological age – and keep it there.

That said, if you can score points on all eight of the items listed in Table 7.1, it will increase your biological age by exactly 7.8 years. The "age me quickly" strategy will take a chronological 58-year-old to the magical age of 65, biologically, and entitle them to an early pension. But would you really do this? I should remind you that while your pension payments will have been accelerated, it is because your life expectancy is now (much) shorter. In other words, you get the money sooner, but it won't last very long.

This might also be a good place to mention that *early* retirement increases your mortality rate and reduces your life expectancy, according to a recently released study by the U.S. National Bureau of Economic Research (although the study was based on Austrian retirees, so who knows).

Again, the number of years you will be drawing this pension will be reduced and it's quite likely that, on a present value (economic) basis, you will have lost. Moreover, if your plan is to get off the "age me quickly" diet as soon the pension is approved, I should remind you that it might not be as easy as you think. I'm sure the system could be set up so as to monitor retirees who suddenly locate the fountain of biological youth soon after starting their pension annuity.

My point is that I just don't envision this sort of *moral hazard*, which is a phrase that academic economists use to describe (and worry about) the process of engaging in activities that willfully distort the probabilities used to price the insurance policy. Yes, consumers might act neglectfully and leave the door open or the house unlocked when they have insurance, but it's a far cry from that casual negligence to permanently harming your body for the sake of an early pension payment. Just as importantly, the same logic would apply to underwritten or impaired life annuities, which is a product that should gain more appeal and traction in a world of growing heterogenous mortality.

In fact, the incentives and nudges – to modify your biological age – would be in the exact opposite direction. By increasing public awareness around the factors that affect healthy aging, and the natural inclination or desire to be younger the older you get, the more likely it is people will try to shy away from claiming early.

Now, whether or not this weighty hypothesis of mine holds true if such a system is adopted, is speculative at this point and remains to be seen. But I don't think it's in the realm of science fiction.

Another Way to Think

The bigger issue, I concede, is not whether the system itself could be gamed by eager pensioners but whether science itself can be relied upon to deliver a biological age number that everyone could and would agree on. If this were to become a global reality, some organizations would have to set standards – no different from the size of an electrical outlet, the periodic table or barcodes – for how to measure and report biological age. Recall that in chapter #5 I described two very different philosophies, that is a "living" versus a "dying" approach, let alone the methodological variations within each paradigm. Could everyone come to an agreement about true biological age? Or on a more fundamental level, does your body have one true age? Perhaps the individual organs or components have different ages? For example, as a chronological 50-year-old, your spleen might be a sprightly and energetic 30-year-old, your lungs might be 50 as well, but your liver – oh my, that liver – is not a day under 90.

I'm only half joking when I write this. There is a company in Korea (south, of course) that uses techniques similar to the ones I described in chapter #5 to estimate the biological age of the vital organs in your body. The company then averages these numbers to arrive at a comprehensive biological age, presumably using some complex weighting procedure. (I can't help but wonder, what gets more weight? Is it the lung or the liver?) This particular company is trying to sell this approach to insurance companies around the world, looking for more efficient and reliable underwriting procedures.

So, perhaps the better way to think about the matter is to leave biological age itself as *random*. It has an average value, a standard deviation as well as higher moments that determine the nature of its uncertainty. You might be 60 years old chronologically and be informed that your expected biological age is 58, with a standard deviation of 10 years. So, you might be as young as 48 biologically, or as old as 68 biologically. *We just don't know for sure.*

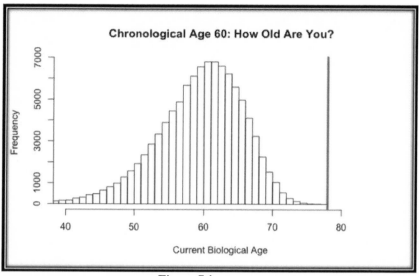

Figure 7.1

Figure 7.1 offers a graphical view of this notion, which I believe is likely the best way to think about the matter. Your chronological age is a fixed and known number, which increases linearly in time. In contrast, your biological age is a *stochastic process*, to use a term favored by applied mathematicians. To push this even further, under this view of the world, your biological age of death is also fixed and known, say 78. You die the first time your biological age "hits" or reaches the age of 78, or more precisely at a biological age at which the mortality rate is such that death is imminent.

You might be 10, 20 or perhaps even 40 years away from death, because your true biological age could be 70, 60 or even 40. As the science improves, you might be able to narrow the uncertainty associated with your biological age. Visually this would imply a shrinking or reduction in the dispersion (standard deviation) of the density in Figure 7.1, but there is always an element of randomness.

You can "improve" on this randomness by either shifting the curve to the left – eating better, exercising regularly and staying away from all the other bad things I noted – or by cutting off the tail risk.

You can work on reducing the randomness by reducing the chances you are much older than your chronological age.

Working with Human Capital

As an author of over 10 books and hundreds of assorted articles, I have learned by now that every published piece has two sacred areas: the beginning and the end. The first few pages and the last few pages are likely the most important parts because they are read. In fact, you can bury almost anything in between the two extremes, and here we are at the end.

Perhaps the ultimate form of *longevity insurance for a biological age* is to voluntarily work for longer, possibly much longer, and then spend less time in retirement. Yes, I know this sounds rather cliché and you have heard about this before. But every additional year working in the labor force generates additional income from what economists call your human capital. The income then goes towards supplementing and growing your nest egg, effectively increasing its longevity. It's two birds with one stone by spending less time in retirement drawing down assets. All reasonable, you say. The problem, of course, is that the chronological ages of 62 or 65 or 67 are very heavy metal "anchors" in our collective mind. Perhaps the significance and merit of your biological age is the ultimate realization that the value of human capital is most sensitive to our continued good health and fortune. That is what should be insured.

End with a Classy Game

One of the graduate courses I teach at our university's business school is an advanced finance elective for executives on the topic of wealth management over the human lifecycle, also referred to as personal finance. In the early part of the 12-week semester, I discuss topics such as human capital valuation, optimal debt management, income tax strategies and insurance product allocation. Towards the end of the term I get to the topic of retirement income planning. I begin that particular lecture with a game, one that I would like to describe here because I really do believe everyone should contemplate playing it when they get closer to their golden years. Here's how it works.

After the students arrive at the lecture hall at the start of class, I hand every one of them 60 poker chips, similar to the ones you might find in a casino. These chips are the same color, size and denomination, identical in all regards. When they sit down at their tables, they also find a small cardboard box in front of them, similar to a large matchbox. The box is separated into six compartments, and each one of them has a label. The first compartment on the very left-hand side is labeled "70 to 75," the second compartment next to it is labeled "75 to 80," all the way to the final compartment on the right-most side that reads "95 to 100."

I inform the students that they should consider each of these compartments or slots as representing five years of their retirement and all six of them together as the entire 30 years. It starts at the age of 70 (chronologically) and ends at the age of 100 (chronologically, as well).

The main point of the entire exercise is for them to imagine these chips as representing their nest egg (i.e. retirement savings, pension pot, etc.), and I ask them to allocate these 60 chips across the six slots in a manner that best represents how they would personally like to spend and spread them over their retirement years.

Now, just to be clear, these aren't 22-year-old undergraduates in the course. Those kids might view the concept of retirement the same way a 50-year-old would view a mosh pit at a rock concert – that is, alien and unappealing. My audience is made up of senior executives in their 40s, for whom retirement planning is visibly on the horizon. They have likely contemplated these things, but perhaps not quite in the way I described.

Back to the chips. Before the students allocate their precious chips into the slots, I reassure them that these are real spending chips. They are meant to be used for expenses that give them pleasure and joy in retirement, not anxiety. I tell them to assume that the stressful stuff like medical care has been fully insured and will be covered by someone else. Again, these chips are for enjoyment.

How would you like to spend them?

I give them a few minutes to think about it, and perhaps debate and consult with a few people at their small classroom tables, then make a decision. I then ask to see what they've done and have them describe their chip allocations. Interestingly enough, and perhaps you might have suspected this, very few students in the class divide the chips evenly across the three decades and allocate 5 chips to each of the identical 6 slots. The boring answer of 60/6 is quite rare.

On a side note, splitting the 60 chips evenly across the retirement slots is the essence of the so-called 4% rule. Technically, allocating 10 chips per five-year bucket works out to 2 chips per year, which is about 3.33% of your initial 60 chip nest egg. Again, nobody does that – at least when I ask them how they would like to actually spend their chips. Perhaps this is worth noting.

Rather, what tends to happen in this game is quite different from 10, 10, 10, etc. And, I suspect the reason it's different is because I remind the students, just before they start placing their chip bets, that longevity isn't a certainty. Longevity is risky, as I have emphasized over and over again.

As a typical or average 40-year-old in my advanced class, the chances they reach the first slot in the box is quite high, perhaps even greater than 95%. But, the odds or probability of reaching that final box – the one that says 95 to 100 – are quite small. Recall from chapter #5 the discussion about the Gompertz law of mortality and the exponentially increasing force of mortality.

Now, I can't say for certain what their probabilities of hitting 100 are without knowing more about them and their biological age, but I would say that generally speaking the probability is less than 5%. With those slim odds, how many chips will they allocate to that slot?

Here is the bottom line. My loud and careful reminder of longevity risk makes this risk salient for them, at least for a few minutes, which leads to a chip allocation similar to the one you see in Figure 7.2. The last box only has three (on average), and the numbers increase as you move backwards and to the left.

Now, to be clear, the numbers I'm displaying are sample averages across the many classes I have taught but notice again that the last slot only receives an allocation of 3 chips. The slot next to it, which represents ages 90 to 95, and associated with a slightly higher probability, receives an average of 7 slots, and so on and so forth until the left-most slot has an allocation of 16 chips. Remember, they all must add up to 60 chips. You can't leave any chips on the table (outside the box) or overspend your chips. By the way, this is precisely why I use physical chips for this retirement income game. When I ask students to imagine chips and slots, the numbers rarely add up to 60 (and I'm only half-joking here).

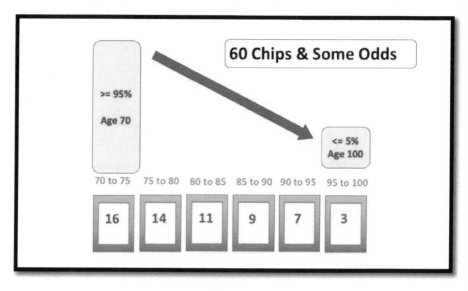

Figure 7.2

Now, to be very clear, not everyone in the class allocates their chips in the 16-14-11-9-7-3 pattern that is displayed in Figure 7.2.

The variation is enormous. Some students allocate more chips in the latter years – they can't imagine living on only three chips – while others front load more of them to the early years, when they are more likely to be alive (and can enjoy them). A few participants implemented an inverted U-shaped pattern, which is quite different from the (average) declining pattern exhibited in Figure 7.2. The inverse-U crowd spend more in the first few years (travel, live-it-up in the "go go" years) as well as the last few years (to die with dignity is expensive). But, in the middle they expect to slow down. Hence, the middle slots are allocated the least chips.

I interpret these variations or heterogeneity across my class and audiences as reflecting their unique preferences as well as longevity risk aversion. Some people really worry about living to a very advanced age and therefore provision more to that scenario regardless of how small the probabilities might be. Others are more longevity-risk tolerant, perhaps no different than investment-risk tolerant when it comes to financial markets and asset allocation. Indeed, one size (preferences) doesn't fit all. Everyone is different and unique. There are billions of different ways to allocate chips.

In fact, once a student of mine took their entire 60 chips and instead of spreading them across the six boxes, placed all 60 of them on the final slot, representing ages 95 to 100. Going from left to right his allocation was zero, zero, zero, zero, zero, 60. Now, when the class noticed this chip allocation, everyone laughed heartily, and perhaps that was his intention. But, when I asked him what he expected to live on for the first 25 years of retirement, he response was dead serious: "Hey, I have a defined benefit pension at work. Guaranteed income for the rest of my natural life. I don't really need these chips." Perhaps they can go to the kids or something.

It's interesting how a guaranteed pension changes peoples spending habits. They seem to care less about the precious nest egg, versus others whose sole source of income are the chips. Again, not everybody spends the same way. Once a female class member asked me: "Hey, Moshe, who gets these chips if I die before reaching that last box? Will they go to my daughter-in-law!?" This seemed to alarm her. She stated quite loudly that if that was the case, she wasn't going to put any chips in the last slot. This provoked yet mores guffaws of laughter from the class. Well they appeared to be having fun, and I really do learn quite a bit about my audience, just by playing this simple game with them.

But the reason I'm ending with this story is because of what happened one semester, when I repeated this routine exercise with yet another group, the game was upstaged by a few clever students.

As most people in the class were quietly pondering and reflecting how they might allocate their chips, I noticed a small group of four sitting at one table and arguing with each other. It sounded like they were negotiating a deal or business agreement. It got quite loud and when I asked them what was going on, they responded with a very interesting question.

They pointed to that last slot on the right, the one that said 95 to 100. They wanted to know: "Can we allocate our chip as a *table*, as opposed to as an *individual?*" Assuming it was allowed, they explained that their strategy was to collect 3 chips from all 4 participants at the table, and then place the 12 chips collectively into that 95 to 100 slot. Their long-term plan was as follows. If they all survived and reached the final slot – an outcome which is quite unlikely I should add – then the 12 chips they had allocated collectively would be divided among the 4 survivors and they would all get back their 3 chips. That is exactly what they had contributed. No loss there.

But, here comes the clever idea. If only one person survived and reached the final slot, that person would get all 12 chips. If only two participants survived they would each get 6 chips, which is 12 divided by the 2 survivors. And, if 3 people survived, which is also quite rare, the survivors would get 4 chips, which is still better than the 3 they had invested. So, best case scenario, the lucky one gets 12 chips, worst case scenario, they all get 3 chips. They would never get back less than 3. Their questions to me were: "Moshe, is this kosher? Can we play the game this way? Can we allocate collectively instead of individually? We would get extra chips that way."

I was impressed with their ingenuity and replied: "Congratulations. You have discovered longevity risk pooling. You just invented a life annuity." And, by the way, the idea is thousands of years old, so don't run out and file a patent just quite yet. Oh, and the extra chips you get – above and beyond the three allocated – are called mortality credits.

This gave me the opportunity to raise a bigger issue. I asked them and the class, "Why stop at the last slot, representing age 95 to 100? Why not do the same with the one to the left, the one that provides for ages 90 to 95. How about 85 to 90? Moreover, why allocate all or nothing? Perhaps allocate some collectively, as a table via pooling, and some individually."

To press the point, I emphasized that if they were willing to pool, I could make their 60 chips behave like 100 chips. It gets a bit technical and I didn't delve into the math, but they could see the intuition.

They start retirement with 60 chips, but by pooling them they can spend – if they survive – as if they had 100 chips. That's the benefit of pooling longevity risk. It expands the original budget by 40 chips. It's as if you have 40 more chips, per initial 60, on day one.

Now, not everyone – in the class or in real life – was enamored by this collective pooling arrangement. One class member stood up and asked for clarification. "So, if I die, then my tablemates inherit my chips?" When I nodded, he then said: "But I hate my tablemates! I don't want them to get my chips when I die." He paused and then said: "I would rather they go to my daughter-in-law!" (Cue more laughter.)

I made it clear to this student that whatever he decided – collectively or individually – was perfectly fine with me. There was no right or wrong allocation and nobody would coerce him to pool any chips, but he better be able to live within his original budget of 60. If that nest egg wasn't too constraining, there was no need to pool. But if he wanted to spend more, or couldn't make it on the 60 chips, he might have no choice but to pool.

Needless to say, this little pooling wrinkle threw a large wrench into my lecture plans for the day. Some people wondered whether such an agreement, which is called a *tontine*, was legal in real life. Couldn't people start murdering each other? Another younger female (I think her name was Heather) contemplated whether she should move to a table with older males, which would increase the odds of her winning the collective pool. (Really loud guffaws.)

Anyway, this all led to a discussion of fairness and whether chronological age was a good proxy for longevity prospects. Perhaps biological age was a better measure for locating pooling mates and identifying who you should avoid swimming with. Most of the class felt that pools (tables) should be segmented by risk class and that they would never voluntarily agree to sit at a table with someone younger. After all, they would be subsidizing them with these mortality credits.

Despite the many unanswered questions raised and dilemmas identified, by the very end of that particular lecture, the consensus was that it was good practice for everyone to allocate at least a few chips to the longevity pool. This was the case even if they were all mixed together in one big heterogeneous classroom. In fact, as the lecture wound down, some class members went so far as to argue that, in real life, governments should force citizens to allocate a few chips collectively, to prevent indigent members of society reaching that final box – not having saved anything – with absolutely no chips. After all, those mortality credits would represent an effective and cheap way of insuring against a socially undesirable outcome.

I agreed and smiled...

ACKNOWLEDGEMENTS

I would like to end by confessing that I was forced to write this book by a lawyer, or more precisely a group of attorneys. Unfortunately, I don't know their names so I can't acknowledge them in person. No, I'm not joking or being sarcastic. And no, this work isn't part of a legal settlement or court-directed restitution. Rather, this project started its (biological) life as a humble collection of PowerPoint slides, many of which were reproduced in the pages of this book.

You see, a while ago I was asked to deliver a presentation on the topic of retirement income planning to a group of financial advisors employed by a well-known investment bank in the U.S. The main idea or points I was planning to make were that (i) retirees are starting to think differently about their true age and therefore the lifecycle planning process must adapt to a revised definition of age, and (ii) financial advisors should embrace their client's inclination to think of themselves as younger, to position longevity insurance (annuities) as protection against being younger than their chronological age.

Getting back to the attorneys, as anyone who has ever given a presentation in a highly regulated industry can confirm, I had to submit my PowerPoint presentation to the firm's compliance department and get the slides approved before I could step on stage. They wanted to ensure I wasn't misleading the audience or running afoul of securities regulations. All quite reasonable.

But alas, the compliance department did not approve the presentation and returned the file to me with a failing grade, accompanied by many queries. They wanted me to report all sources, cite all references, and – in a request destined to send shudders down the spine of any academic – they wanted *detailed speaking notes*. Groan! That's almost impossible for a university professor who clocks 180 words per minute.

Nevertheless, I wanted to deliver my presentation – and obviously cash the check – so I had no choice but to comply. And, it was an onerous process involving a series of back-and-forth emails with anonymous attorneys, all via an intermediary in the marketing and sales group. In fact, at some point it left like I was dealing with a new person at each iteration as material that was approved in round 4 was suddenly challenged in round 9, etc. Normally I might call up and chat with someone who was confused about a particular point I was trying to make, but the rules of engagement dictated that all of this had to be done in writing. (Not unlike the anonymous peer-review process.) In the end, and just in time, the slide deck was approved and I was granted permission to give my speech.

More importantly, it dawned on me that if I threaded the emails, notes and replies together with a bit of editing I could convert the material into a small book. So, here we are. Thank you, compliance!

On a slightly more serious note, I would like to acknowledge and thank my long-time research collaborators and co-authors Huaxiong Huang and Tom Salisbury, both from the Department of Mathematics and Statistics at York University. We have written many technical articles over the years and, in particular, published an (academic) article "Retirement Spending and Biological Age," which was the impetus for the material in the above-noted presentation.

I also appreciate many conversations with Leonid Gavrilov and Natalia Gavrilova, authors of the classic book *The Biology of Life Span*, which affected much of my thinking on longevity modeling, the Gompertz model and mortality plateaus. In particular, I have fond memories of lunches, dinners and drinks with them in Chicago.

Likewise, I appreciate comments and encouragement from David Blake, Don Ezra, Steven Haberman, Mark Kamstra, Pier-Carl Michaud, Thomas Post, David Promislow, Pauline Shum and audience members at various scholarly conferences. When building a new idea, every little comment (and criticism) helps.

In terms of sources, some housekeeping and disclosures are in order. First, if and when you encounter a number or a table or a fact without an actual source – sorry for the omission – the official source should be listed as the author (i.e. me). I either computed the number myself or hand collected the original data.

Also, some of the material on pensions (chapter #3) appeared in an article I wrote and (is to be) published in the *Journal of Pension Economic and Finance*. Also, an expanded version of the material in the chapter on insurance allocations (chapter #4) – with more on the pros, cons and misconceptions of annuities – was published in the *Journal of Financial Planning* in December 2018. The algorithm for converting country or group-specific mortality rates into "universal" biological ages is described fully in (Milevsky, 2019). Finally, the original technical article which set the stage for biological age "thinking" was published in November 2017 in the *Journal of Economic Dynamics and Control*, cited as (Huang, Milevsky, & Salisbury, 2017). A technical sequel to that work is in progress, to be written by Bushra Ashraf, who is a Ph.D. candidate at York University.

Last, but not least, as far the writing and typesetting is concerned, Andrea MacLeod was indispensable in walking a self-publishing novice through the process of working with Amazon and Kindle. She also designed the lovely cover for the book. I would also like to thank Beth McAuley of The Editing Company in Toronto who gave this final draft of the manuscript a really good polish. Last but certainly not least, thank you to my dear wife Edna, who – as with every other book I have written – carefully read the manuscript and found (too) many typos.

References

Almond, D. (2006, August). Is the 1918 Influenza Pandemic Over? Long-term Effects of In Utero Influenza Exposure in the Post 1940 U.S. Population. *Journal of Political Economy, 114*(4), 672-712.

Arnold, C. (2018). *Pandemic 1918: Eyewitness Accounts from the Greatest Medical Holocaust in Modern History.* New York: St. Martin's Press.

Barry, J. M. (2009). *The Great Influenza: The Epic Story of the Deadliest Plague in History.* London, England: Penguin Books.

Brown, J. (2003). Redistribution and insurance: Mandatory annuitization with mortality heterogeneity. *Journal of Risk and Insurance, 70*(1), 17-41.

Casaburi, L., & Willis, J. (2018). Time versus State in Insurance: Experimental Evidence from Contract Farming in Kenya. *American Economic Review, 108*(12), 3778-3813.

Chetty, R., Stepner, M., Abraham, S., Lin, S., Scuderi, B., Turner, N., . . . Cutler, D. (2016). The association between income and life expectancy in the United States: 2001-2014. *Journal of the American Medical Association, 315*(16), 1750-1766.

Diamond, P. (2004). Social Security: Presidential Address. *American Economic Review, 94*(1), 1-24.

Dubina, T. L., Mints, A. Y., & Zhuk, E. V. (1984). Biological Age and its Estimation. III. Introduction of a Correction to the Multiple Regression Model of Biological Age and Assessment of Biological Age in Cross-Sectional and Longitudinal Studies. *Experimental Gerontology, 19*, 133-143.

Fizzard, A. (2005). Retirement Arrangements and the Laity at Religious Houses in Pre-Reformation Devon. *FLORILEGIUM, 22*, 57-79.

Gagnon, A., Miller, M. S., Hallman, S. A., Bourbeau, R., Herring, D. A., Earn, D. J., & Madrenas, J. (2013). Age-specific Mortality During the 1918 Influenza Pandemic: Unravelling the Mystery of High Young Adult Mortality. *PLOS ONE, 8*(8), 1-9.

Gardner, D. (2008). *RISK: Why We Fear the Things We Shouldn't and Put Ourselves in Greater Danger.* Toronto: McClelland & Stewart.

Gavrilov, L. A., & Gavrilova, N. S. (1991). *The Biology of Lifespan: A Quantitative Approach.* United Kingdom: Harwood Academic Publishers.

Held, G. (2002). Research into the Aging Process: A Survey. *North American Actuarial Journal*, 30-37.

Huang, H., Milevsky, M. A., & Salisbury, T. S. (2017). Retirement Spending and Biological Age. *Journal of Economic Dynamics and Control, 84*, 58-76.

Jackson, S. H., Weale, M. R., & Weale, R. A. (2003). Biological Age: What is it and can it be measured? *Archives of Gerontology and Geriatrics, 36*, 103-115.

Jylhava, J., Pederson, N. L., & Hagg, S. (2017). Biological Age Predictors. *EBioMedicine*, 29-36.

Lewin, C. G. (2003). *Pensions and Insurance Before 1800: A Social History.* East Lothian: Tuckwell Press.

McCrea, M., & Farrell, M. (2018). A Conceptual Model for Pricing Health and Life Insurance Using Wearable Technology. *Risk Management and Insurance Review, 21*(3), 389-411.

Milevsky, M. A. (2005). Real Longevity Insurance with a Deductible: Introduction to Advanced-Life Delayed Annuities (ALDA). *North American Actuarial Journal, 9*(4), 109-122.

Milevsky, M. A. (2012). *The 7 Most Important Equations for Your Retirement: The Fascinating People and Ideas Behind Planning Your Retirement Income.* Toronto: WILEY.

Milevsky, M. A. (2019). Calibrating Gompertz in Reverse: Mortality-adjusted Biological Ages around the World. *Working Paper.*

Milevsky, M. A. (2019). Swimming with Wealthy Sharks: Longevity, Volatility and the Value of Risk Pooling. *Journal of Pension Economics and Finance*, (in press).

Milevsky, M. A., & Macqueen, A. C. (2016). *Pensionize Your Nest Egg: How to Use Product Allocation to Create a Guaranteed Income for Life.* Toronto: WILEY.

Murphy, S. A. (2010). *Investing in Life: Insurance in Antebellum America.* Baltimore: The John Hopkins University Press.

OECD. (2014). *Mortality Assumptions and Longevity Risk: Implications for Pension Funds and Annuity Providers.* Paris: OECD Publishing.

OECD. (2018). *OECD Pensions Outlook 2018.* Paris: OECD Publishing.

Ries, W., & Pothig, D. (1984). Chronological and Biological Age. *Experimental Gerontology, 19*, 211-216.

Shoven, J. B. (2007). New Age Thinking: Alternative Ways of Measuring Age, Their Relationship to Labor Force Participation, Government Policies and GDP. *National Bureau of Economic Reserch Working Paper #13476.*

Shoven, J. B., & Goda, G. S. (2008). Adjusting Government Policies for Age Inflation. *National Bureau of Economic Research Working Paper #14231.*

Stevens, R. (2017). Managing Longevity Risk by Implementing full Retirement Age Policies. *Journal of Risk and Insurance, 84*(4), 1203-1230.

VanDerhi, J. (2019, January). Deferred Income Annuity Purchases: Optimal Levels for Retirement Income Adequacy. *EBRI Issue Brief, 469*, 1-19.

Ye, Z., & Post, T. (2018). What Age Do You Feel? Subjective Age and Economic Behavior. *NETSPAR Working Paper*.

ABOUT THE AUTHOR

Moshe A. Milevsky is a tenured professor at the Schulich School of Business and a member of the graduate faculty in Mathematics and Statistics at York University in Toronto, Canada. He has published 14 books (translated into six languages) and over 60 peer-reviewed scholarly papers in addition to hundreds of popular articles in newspapers and magazines. He is also a very popular speaker who has delivered over 1,000 keynote presentations and seminars around the world. For more information about his research work, please visit his website at www.MosheMilevsky.com

Made in the USA
Middletown, DE
16 April 2019